Japan Incorporation for Foreign Business Owners

和英対照

インバウンド会社設立ガイド

公認会計士・税理士 三宅周兵

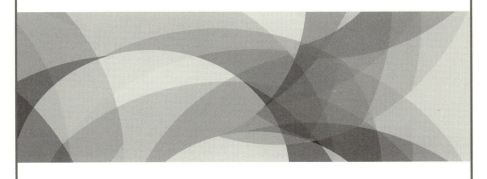

中央経済社

はしがき

　世界銀行が発表したDoing Business 2019によると，「最もビジネスがしやすい国ランキング」で，日本は39位と，他の先進国に比べて非常に低い順位となっています。これはなぜでしょうか。日本社会の閉鎖性や行政手続の複雑さなどがあげられることが多いですが，英語が通用しにくいことも大きな要因の１つだと思います。ビジネスがしやすい国ランキングで常に上位に入るシンガポール（2019年度２位）は，いち早く英語を公用語に採用することで外国資本を呼び込むことに成功し，いまでは１人当たりのGDPが日本を抜いてアジア第１位となっています。シンガポールでは，海外から企業が新たに進出する際に必要となる知識や情報は，事前に英語で容易に入手することができます。

　私が赴任先のシンガポールから日本に戻ってきて改めて気づいたことは，日本の諸制度や法令について，正確な情報が英語で十分に発信されていないということでした。法務省や国税局など政府のホームページにおいて英語で情報を入手することができますが，その情報量は日本語のページと比べて極端に少ないのが現状です。専門家によって書かれた外資系企業向けの書籍も存在しますが，その多くは日本語で書かれています。

　本書は，外資系企業が日本進出を検討するにあたり，事前に本国本社が日本の制度を十分に研究していただけるように，という思いから執筆しました。外資系企業の日本進出を支援しているなかで，本国本社に対して説明している事柄を中心に，実務の観点からQ&A形式でまとめました。

　会社設立に関する書籍のなかには，単に登記手続だけを説明したものも少なくありません。事業を始めるにはヒト・モノ・カネを取りそろえる必要がありますが，日本で商品・サービスを販売するために，どのように現地の人材をコントロールしていくかというコーポレートガバナンスの問題，どのように資金を調達するかというファイナンスの問題にも取り組む必要があります。ヒトとカネの２大生産要素をどのように調達し運用していく

1

かの大枠は，会社設立の段階で設計しておかなければなりません。そのため，本書では，コーポレートガバナンスとファイナンスに焦点を当てています。

コーポレートガバナンスの章では，取締役の権限，義務および責任の解説に紙面を割きました。日本で採用した経営者が海外の本社の目を盗んで不正を行うリスクについて，本社は事前に認識し，会社組織を構築していくなかで対策を講じておくことが重要です。そのためには，取締役の競業避止義務など，不正防止に有効な法令について理解しておくことが有益です。ファイナンスの章では，税負担がなるべく少なくなるようなストラクチャーを構築するために，配当や売却など一連の投資サイクルにおける税のインパクトを中心に解説しました。

執筆にあたって，日本特有の制度について丁寧な解説を心がけました。例えば，株式会社の監査役は日本独自の制度であり，外国の方にとって馴染みがなく，理解するのが難しいようなので，正しく理解していただけるようわかりやすい説明に努めました。

本書が，本国本社の経営陣，法務部門，財務部門，日本法人の責任者，バックオフィスの方々，外資系企業の支援に携わる実務家の方々，日本の会社制度に関する理解を必要とするすべての皆さまの一助となれば幸いです。

令和元年9月1日

公認会計士・税理士

三 宅 周 兵

はしがき　Preface

Preface

According to the "Ease of Doing Business Ranking" conducted by World Bank in their report "Doing Business 2019", Japan was placed the 39th among 190 countries, which is the worst among developed countries.

I've been thinking about what made Japan rank so low while we have the 3rd largest market in the world. Some people say it's because Japan is still a very closed society, and others say it's due to regulatory complexity. I think one big factor is that most Japanese do not speak English.

Singapore, where I used to live, is a great contrast to Japan since it is always ranked among the top three in the World Bank's report. Singapore adopted English as its official language, and it has been the working language for the governments and businesses since it started its modern history, and the government has always been making great efforts to attract foreign corporations. Now, Singapore is ranked at the top among Asia countries in GDP Per Capita ranking, and there is no doubt that the use of English has contributed to their economic success. It is quite easy for foreign corporations who wish to enter the Singapore market to obtain information and knowledge in English about local business environment and regulations.

When I returned to Japan after my assignment in Singapore, I realized that it's very difficult to find accurate and useful information about Japanese laws and regulations published in English. There are some tax and legal information available in English on the government's websites such as the Ministry of Justice and the National Tax Agency. However, the amount of information is very few compared to the Japanese pages. There are books out there written by professionals for foreign corporations, but most of them are written in Japanese.

This is why I decided to write this book for people at head offices who want to research on local laws and regulations before entering the

Japan market. I picked up some major questions which I get asked from headquarters that want to set up a new frontier fort in Japan.

I've noticed that many books on incorporation just describe the registration procedures of a company. However, there are things you need to consider before registration. When starting a new business, you need to prepare three key elements for your business: product to sell, people to work with, and money. You should learn how to control your local workforce and how to fund your local entity before you bring your products into the new market. That is why I focused on corporate governance and finance in this book.

In the chapter of corporate governance, I put emphasis on powers, duties and responsibilities of company directors. It is crucial for head offices to realize that there is always a risk that local directors might conduct fraud transactions behind you, and that it is important to consider preventive measures when you design the corporate governance structure. It's beneficial to know there are preventive clauses in the Companies Act such as prohibition on competition by directors.

In the chapter of finance, I focused on tax implications on financial transactions such as dividends and selling shares, which will help you design a tax efficient structure.

I also put a detailed explanation about systems which are unique to Japan. For example, I explained plainly about Corporate Auditors which may be unfamiliar to foreigners and difficult to understand.

I hope this book will help top management, legal and financial department at headquarters, local management and back office at Japan offices, professionals supporting foreign corporations, and all others who are in need to understand the Japanese company system more deeply.

Joey Shuhei Miyake
CPA, CPTA
September 1, 2019

目　　次
Contents

はしがき　*1*
Preface　*3*

Chapter　1　事業体の選択
Business Entity ——————————— *1*

▶▶**事業体の種類** ————————————————————— *2*

Q1　日本でビジネスを始めるにあたってどのような事業形態が利用で
きますか。……………………………………………………… *2*
What types of business entities are available to start a
business in Japan? …………………………………………… *3*

Q2　駐在員事務所はどのような事務所ですか。……………………… *6*
What is a representative office? ………………………… *7*

Q3　支店はどのような事務所ですか。………………………………… *10*
What is a branch office? …………………………………… *11*

Q4　株式会社とはどのような会社ですか。…………………………… *14*
What is a Kabushiki Kaisha (K.K.)？ …………………… *15*

Q5　合同会社はどのような会社ですか。……………………………… *18*
What is a Godo Kaisha (G.K.)？ ………………………… *19*

▶▶**事業体を比較検討する際のポイント** ———————————— *20*

Q6　事業形態によって税金の負担は異なりますか。………………… *20*
Does the tax implication differ between types of
business entity? ……………………………………………… *21*

Q7　本国の親会社は日本事業から生じた債務に責任を負いますか。……… *24*
Is the parent company in the home country responsible
for the debt of Japanese business? …………………… *25*

Q8　経営者は日本に居住している必要がありますか。……………… *26*

I

Does a director need to live in Japan? ································ *27*

Q9 資本金の金額はどのように決定しますか。 ···················· *28*
How is the amount of capital determined? ···················· *29*

Q10 資本金の額が要件となる優遇税制はありますか。 ················ *32*
Are there any tax advantages available for companies
with a small capital amount? ································ *33*

Q11 役員に対する報酬は税務上の費用となりますか。 ················ *38*
Are fees for officers and directors tax deductible? ··········· *39*

Q12 日本から事業を撤退させるにはどのような方法がありますか。 ······ *40*
How do you close down your business in Japan ? ·············· *41*

Chapter 2 **PEストラクチャー**
PE Structure ———————————— *45*

Q13 「PE無ければ課税無し」はどのような原則ですか。 ·············· *46*
What does "No Tax Without PE" mean ? ···················· *47*

Q14 支店はPEに該当しますか。 ································ *48*
Is a branch office a PE? ································ *49*

Q15 外国法人の施設がPEにあたらないケースはありますか。 ·········· *50*
Are there any exemptions from PE? ························ *51*

Q16 日本で課税される支店の利益はどのように算定しますか。 ·········· *56*
How are the profits of the branch measured? ················ *57*

Q17 子会社はPEに該当しますか。 ······························ *58*
Can a subsidiary create a PE? ···························· *59*

Q18 コミッショネア方式で親会社の商品を売買していますがPEに
該当しますか。 ·· *60*
If a subsidiary is selling products purchased from its
foreign parent company under the contract of
commissionaire, is the subsidiary deemed as a PE? ··········· *61*

Q19 コストプラスカンパニーとはどのような会社ですか。 ·············· *64*
What's a cost-plus company? ······························ *65*

Q20 外国親会社から日本の子会社が商品を輸入する際，仕入値はど
のように決定すれば良いですか。 ·························· *66*

目 次 CONTENTS

How do you determine the purchase price when
a subsidiary imports the goods from its foreign parent? ···· *67*

Chapter 3 コーポレートガバナンス
Corporate Governance ——————— *69*

▶▶コーポレートガバナンスとは ————————————— *70*

Q21 コーポレートガバナンスとは何ですか。·· *70*
What is corporate governance? ··· *71*

Q22 コーポレートガバナンスは事業形態によってどのように異なり
ますか。··· *72*
How does corporate governance vary between business
entities? ··· *73*

Q23 日本の事業に対してどのようなコーポレートガバナンスを構築
すべきですか。··· *74*
What kind of corporate governance should be established
for the operation in Japan? ································· *75*

▶▶株式会社のコーポレートガバナンス ————————— *76*

▶コーポレートガバナンスの類型 ————————————— *76*

Q24 「取締役会設置会社」とはどのような会社ですか。····················· *76*
What is a "Company with Board of Directors"? ··············· *77*

Q25 「取締役会非設置会社」とはどのような会社ですか。····················· *80*
What is a "Company without Board of Directors"? ············· *81*

Q26 「株式譲渡制限会社」とはどのような会社ですか。····················· *82*
What is a "Private Company"? ································· *83*

▶株主および株主総会 ——————————————————— *84*

Q27 株主にはどのような権利が与えられ，どのような義務および責任を
負っていますか。··· *84*
What rights, obligations and responsibilities do
shareholders have? ··· *85*

Q28 株主総会にはどのような権限がありますか。····························· *86*
What powers does a shareholders' meeting have? ············· *87*

III

Q29	株主総会はどうやって招集しますか。	88
	How is a shareholders' meeting convened?	89
Q30	株主総会に外国親会社が実際に出席する必要はありますか。	90
	Does a parent company have to attend a shareholders' meeting?	91
Q31	株主総会はどうやって決議を行いますか。	92
	How does a shareholders' meeting pass resolutions?	93

▶取締役 ——————————————————— 94

Q32	取締役にはどのような権限がありますか。	94
	What powers do directors have?	95
Q33	取締役の選任・解任はどのように行いますか。	96
	How are directors elected and dismissed?	97
Q34	取締役の報酬はどうやって決めますか。	98
	How to determine the amounts of remuneration for directors?	99
Q35	取締役が負う一般義務とはどのような義務ですか。	100
	What are the general duties of directors?	101
Q36	取締役が負う「競業避止義務」とはどのような義務ですか。	102
	What is directors' "Non compete obligation"?	103
Q37	取締役による「利益相反取引」とは何ですか。	104
	What is directors' "Conflict-of-interest transactions"?	105
Q38	取締役は会社に対してどのような責任を負いますか。	108
	What makes directors liable to the company?	109
Q39	株主は違法行為をした取締役を訴えることができますか？	112
	Are shareholders able to sue directors for wrongful acts?	113
Q40	取締役は会社が第三者に与えた損害に対して直接責任を負いますか。	114
	Are directors liable to third parties for damages caused by the company？	115

▶取締役会 ——————————————————— 116

| Q41 | 取締役会にはどのような権限が与えられていますか。 | 116 |

IV

目 次 CONTENTS

What powers does a board of directors have? ················· *117*

Q42 取締役会はどうやって招集しますか。 ················· *118*
How to convene a board meeting? ····························· *119*

Q43 取締役会はどうやって決議を行いますか。 ················· *120*
How does a board of directors make a decision? ··········· *121*

▶代表取締役 ————————————————————————— *122*

Q44 代表取締役にはどのような権限が与えられていますか。 ············· *122*
What powers do representative directors have? ············· *123*

Q45 代表権とはどのような権限ですか。 ····························· *124*
What is the "authority to represent the company"? ········· *125*

Q46 取締役会の決議を経ないで代表取締役が行った取引は無効にな
りますか。 ··· *126*
If a representative director makes a deal without
a necessary resolution of the board of directors, is the
deal deemed as void? ··· *127*

▶監査役 ———————————————————————————— *128*

Q47 監査役とはどのような役職ですか。 ····························· *128*
What is a Corporate Auditor? ································· *129*

Q48 監査役はどのような職務を行いますか。 ························· *130*
What duties do Corporate Auditors have? ··················· *131*

Q49 監査役の選任・解任はどのように行いますか。 ················· *132*
How are Corprate Auditors elected and dismissed? ········· *133*

▶▶合同会社のコーポレートガバナンス ————————————— *134*

Q50 合同会社のコーポレートガバナンスの特徴はなんでしょうか。 ····· *134*
How is G.K. governed? ··· *135*

Q51 業務執行社員はどのような義務を負いますか。 ················· *136*
What duties do executive members have? ··················· *137*

▶▶支店のコーポレートガバナンス ————————————————— *138*

Q52 支店のコーポレートガバナンスの特徴は何でしょうか。 ············· *138*
How is a branch of foreign corporation governed? ··········· *139*

V

Q53 日本における代表者とはどういう役職ですか。 *140*
What is a Representative of Japan? *141*

Chapter 4 ファイナンス
Finance Structure ——————— *143*

▶▶ファイナンス ————————————————— *144*

Q54 日本拠点へ事業資金を投下する際に検討すべきポイントは何ですか。 *144*
What needs to be considered when investing in
a business in Japan? *145*

Q55 移転価格税制とはどのような税制ですか。 *146*
What Is Transfer Pricing Taxation? *147*

Q56 過少資本税制とはどのような税制ですか。 *148*
What is Thin Capitalization Rules? *149*

Q57 過大支払利子税制とはどのような税制ですか。 *152*
What is Earnings Stripping Rules? *153*

Q58 国際間の貸付金の利息にはどのような税金がかかりますか。 *154*
What taxes will be imposed on interest on international
loans? *155*

Q59 国際間の配当には日本でどのような税金がかかりますか。 *156*
What taxes will be imposed on international
dividends? *157*

Q60 配当の国際二重課税を回避する方法はありますか。 *158*
How to avoid international double taxation
on dividends? *159*

Q61 配当せず留保した場合にどのような税金がかかりますか。 *162*
What taxes will be imposed if the company does not
distribute earnings as dividends and keep them as
retained earnings? *163*

Q62 日本法人の株式または持分を譲渡すると日本でどのような税金がかかりますか。 *166*
What taxes will be incurred in Japan when selling
shares or equity interests in a Japanese company? *167*

VI

目　次 CONTENTS

▶▶株式会社のファイナンス ———————————— *170*

Q63 借入金で資金を調達するにはどのような手続が必要になりますか。 *170*
What procedures are required for debt financing? *171*

Q64 新株を発行して増資するにはどのような手続が必要になりますか。 *172*
What procedures are required to issue new shares for equity funding? *173*

Q65 赤字であっても配当することはできますか。 *176*
Is a company allowed to distribute dividends when the company made losses? *177*

Q66 株式を譲渡するにはどのような手続が必要になりますか。 *178*
What procedures are required when I sell shares? *179*

Q67 会社が株主から株式を取得することはできますか。 *180*
Can a company buy back shares from shareholders? *181*

Q68 会社に対して株式を譲渡するとどのような税金がかかりますか。 *182*
What taxes will be imposed if I sell my shares to the company? *183*

▶▶合同会社のファイナンス ———————————— *184*

Q69 新たな出資者を追加して資金調達するにはどのような手続が必要になりますか。 *184*
What procedures are required to add a new member and inject new money? *185*

Q70 合同会社の配当はどのように行われますか。 *186*
How does G.K. distribute dividends? *187*

Q71 持分の譲渡はどのような手続が必要になりますか。 *188*
What procedures will be required for selling equity in G.K.? *189*

Q72 社員は出資金の一部を払い戻すことはできますか。 *190*
Can members claim a refund of their investment amount in G.K.? *191*

Q73 社員を辞めて持分全額を払い戻すことはできますか。 *192*

VII

Can I quit being a member of G.K. and claim a refund of the full amount of equity? ··· *193*

▶▶支店のファイナンス ─────────────────── *194*

Q74 支店が本店から資金の供給を受ける際に検討すべきポイントは何ですか。 ··· *194*
What needs to be considered when a branch office is financed by the head office? ······································· *195*

Chapter 5 設立手続 Incorporation ──────────── *197*

▶▶株式会社 ─────────────────────────── *198*

Q75 最低株主数および最低資本金の規制はありますか。 ·············· *198*
Are there minimum requirements for the capital amount and the number of shareholders? ······················ *199*

Q76 株式会社の設立の流れについて教えてください。 ················· *200*
What are the steps to incorporating K.K.? ················· *201*

Q77 会社名を決める際に検討すべきポイントは何ですか。 ·········· *206*
What needs to be considered when naming a new company? ·· *207*

Q78 定款には何を記載しますか。 ································· *208*
What do the articles of incorporation describe? ··············· *209*

Q79 登記にはどのような情報が開示されますか。 ··················· *212*
What information does the company register disclose? ·· *213*

Q80 日本に外資規制はありますか。 ······························· *214*
Does Japan have foreign investment restrictions? ·········· *215*

▶▶合同会社 ─────────────────────────── *218*

Q81 最低社員数および最低資本金の規制はありますか。 ·············· *218*
Are there minimum requirements for the capital amount and the number of members? ························· *219*

目　次 CONTENTS

Q82 合同会社の設立の流れについて教えてください。 ……………………… *220*
What are the steps to incorporating G.K.? ……………………… *221*

▶▶支　　店 ——————————————————————————— *222*

Q83 支店の登記の流れについて教えてください。 ……………………… *222*
How do I register Japan branch of foreign
corporation? ……………………………………………… *223*

Chapter **6** 現地税制
Local Taxation ——————————————— *225*

Q84 法人税の概要について教えてください。 ……………………………… *226*
What taxes will be imposed on corporate incomes? ……… *227*

Q85 消費税はどのような税制ですか。 ………………………………………… *230*
What is Consumption tax? ……………………………………… *231*

Q86 消費税の課税事業者となる要件は何ですか。 ……………………… *232*
What are C-tax registration thresholds? ……………………… *233*

Q87 日本ではどのような取引に源泉所得税が課せられますか。 ………… *236*
What payments are subject to withholding tax in Japan?
……………………………………………………………… *237*

IX

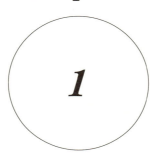

事業体の選択
Business Entity

▶▶事業体の種類

> **Q1　日本でビジネスを始めるにあたってどのような事業形態が利用できますか。**

A　一般的に，支店，株式会社，合同会社の3つの事業形態が利用されています。事業を開始する前に駐在員事務所を置いて市場調査を行う場合もあります。

　支店は外国法人から独立した法人ではなく，外国法人の登録事務所です。外国企業が直接日本で事業を行う場合は，外国企業の情報を登記して一般に公開する必要があります。

　これに対して，本国の外国会社から法的に独立した法人を設立して事業を行う方法が考えられます。営利活動を行う法人として会社があります。会社には，合名会社，合資会社，株式会社および合同会社の4種類があります。そのなかで最も一般的に利用されている会社形態は株式会社です。その理由として，第1に，株式会社は有限責任会社であり，出資者である株主は会社の債務から保護されていることがあげられます。もう1つの理由は，株式会社がもつレピュテーションの高さにあります。株式会社はもともと多くの投資家が出資する会社として設計されており，強固なコーポレートガバナンス構造を構築する必要がある大企業によって使用されていました。2006年の会社法改正で，柔軟に組織やルールを変更できるようになり，小規模な事業者でも利用可能となったのちも，株式会社の形態はその社会的認知度と信用力を保っています。

　2006年に導入された新しい会社形態である合同会社は，パートナーシップの性格をもった有限責任会社です。すなわち，出資者が自ら経営を行うことを想定した会社でありながら，株式会社と同様に出資者は会社の債務から保護されています。アメリカのLLCと似ていますが，日本の国内税法ではパススルー課

Chapter One：事業体の選択 Business Entity

Q1 What types of business entities are available to start a business in Japan?

A Popular forms for business are a branch office, Kabushiki Kaisha (K.K.) and Godo Kaisha (G.K.). Also, a representative office might be chosen to conduct market research before starting a business.

A branch office is a registered office of a foreign corporation, not a separate legal entity from its parent entity. When foreign companies directly do business in Japan, it is required to register its information and make it available to the public.

A company is a separate legal entity for business use. The Companies Act provides four types of companies, Goshi Kaisha, Gomei Kaisha, Godo Kaisha (G.K.) and Kabushiki Kaisha (K.K.). The most popular form is K.K. Firstly, K.K. is a limited company, protecting shareholders from the company's liabilities. Secondly, K.K. has great reputation. Since K.K. is originally designed as a company with a number of investors, it had been chosen by big corporations who need to build up robust corporate governance structures. As a result of the Companies Act Reform 2006, K.K. became available for small businesses, providing great flexibility to design structures and rules, and still reputable in Japan today.

The 2006 Reform also introduced a new type of company. Godo-Kaisha (G.K.) is a limited company with partnership characters. Investors will join the management of the company while they are protected from company's liabilities. Although G.K. has similar characteristics to LLC in US, pass-through taxation — taxation imposed on an investor rather than an entity —

3

税（事業体ではなく出資者に対して所得税を課す課税方式）は認められていません。

　そのほか，支店や会社を設立して事業を始める前に，市場に近い場所で調査を行うために日本に未登記の事務所を開設することがあります。市場調査など補助的な活動を行うために外国会社が設置する事務所を一般的に駐在員事務所と呼びます。

Chapter One：事業体の選択 Business Entity

is not available under Japan domestic tax laws.

Before setting up a branch office or a company, you may want to set up a non-registered office in Japan to conduct market research to understand the market beforehand. This office is known as a representative office, which is supposed to conduct auxiliary and preparatory activities including market research.

Q2 駐在員事務所はどのような事務所ですか。

A 駐在員事務所とは，事業を始める前に市場調査など補助的な活動を行うために外国会社が設置する事務所です。登記や届出など設置の手続は不要で，収益獲得活動を行わないため法人税はかかりません。

市場調査など補助的な活動を行うために外国会社が設置する事務所を，一般的に駐在員事務所といいます。駐在員事務所は支店として登記を行わない以上は収益を伴う直接的営業活動を行うことはできません。外国会社の事務所が「日本において取引を継続してする」（会社法818条）には，外国会社は当該事務所を支店として登記し，外国会社の支店に関する規制に従う必要があります。

日本では，駐在員事務所それ自体を規律する法規制はなく，銀行や保険会社を除き，設置にあたって登記や届出など特段の手続は必要ありません。

また，駐在員事務所は収益活動を行わないため，法人税の申告を行う義務はありません。

一方で，登記を行わないので，日本で存在を証明する証明書である商業登記簿謄本が発行されません。また，日本での取引においてサインの代わりによく用いられる代表者印の印鑑登録もできません。そのため，オフィスの賃貸借契約など重要な契約を締結する際に，取引相手先から本国の公文書およびその翻訳が求められることがあります。賃貸人は，手続が面倒になるというだけの理由で，駐在員事務所への貸出しを拒否することがあります。

Chapter One：事業体の選択 Business Entity

Q2　What is a representative office?

A　A representative office is an office established by a foreign company to conduct market research and other auxiliary activities before starting a business in Japan. There are no legal registration requirements for representative offices. Since representative offices do not engage in sales activities, they are not subject to corporate income tax.

An office established by a foreign company to engage in activities such as conducting market research and feasibility studies is generally called a representative office. Representative offices are prohibited from conducting direct profit-making activities unless it is registered as a branch office. The Companies Act requires a foreign company to register its office as a branch and to be in compliance with the branch office regulations when it intends to "carry out transactions continuously in Japan" (the Companies Act Article 818).

In Japan, there are no laws or regulations that governs representative offices, except for banks and insurance companies. Neither registration nor notification are necessary for setting an office. Since representative offices are intended as a non-profitable facility, it has no obligation to file tax returns for corporate income tax.

On the other hand, a Certified copy of commercial registration — an official certificate to prove the presence in Japan — is not available, because a representative office is not registered under corporate law. Also, you cannot use a Registered representative's seal — an official seal often used instead of signature for authorizing documents in Japan. If you don't have the seal, you may encounter difficulties when you make an important deal like office rent agreements. Your counterpart may ask you for official

7

さらには，日本で登記を行っていない外国法人は，日本の銀行で口座を開設することができません。そのため，駐在員が個人の名義に駐在員事務所の屋号をつけて口座開設することがあります。

Chapter One：事業体の選択 Business Entity

certificates issued by the home government with its Japanese translation instead. Lessors sometimes even refuse to rent out to representative offices just because you don't have a registered representative seal.

Furthermore, a foreign corporation that has not registered in Japan cannot open an account in a Japanese bank. The expatriate may open a personal bank account and add the office name next to his/her name.

Q3 支店はどのような事務所ですか。

A 支店とは，外国会社が日本で事業を行う場合に設置する営業所です。外国会社の日本における代表者を定める必要があり，そのうち1人以上は日本に住所を有している必要があります。

外国会社が日本に設けた営業所を一般的に日本支店といいます。外国会社は，日本において継続して取引を行う場合は，日本における代表者を定め，登記する必要があります（会社法817条，818条）。日本における代表者のうち，1人以上は，日本に住所を有している必要があります。

2002年の法改正以前は，日本において継続して取引を行う場合は，物理的な営業所の設置が義務づけられていましたが，電子商取引の進展から，営業所の設置は義務ではなくなりました。逆に言うと，日本に支店を設置していなくても，電子商取引によって日本で継続的に取引を行う場合には，外国会社は日本における代表者を定めて登記する必要があります。

支店は外国会社の一部分であり，日本支店の負債は外国企業が直接責任を持つため，強い財政基盤や信用力を持つ外国会社は，支店のほうが債権者に信頼を与えることができます。一方で，日本のビジネスパートナーや業者のなかには，日本に設立された会社のほうが日本市場へ強いコミットメントを示しているように思われるという理由だけで，支店よりも株式会社や合同会社のほうを好む人もいます。

外国会社が支店を設けて事業を行う場合は，基本的には恒久的施設（PE: Permanent Establishment）に該当するため，法人税など利益を課税標準とする税金の対象になり，税務署へ支店開設の届出を行う必要があります。日本支

Chapter One：事業体の選択 Business Entity

$Q3$ What is a branch office?

A A branch office is a sales office of a foreign company that is established when a foreign company conducts a business in Japan. It is required to appoint a Japan representative(s) of the foreign company, and at least one of the representatives must be domiciled in Japan.

Sales offices established by foreign companies in Japan are generally called Japan branches. Foreign companies need to appoint and register a representative(s) in Japan, if they conduct their business continuously in Japan (the Companies Act Article 817 and 818). At least one representative must have an address in Japan.

Before the reform in 2002, foreign companies were required to establish its physical sales office when they conduct transactions in Japan continuously. With development and expansion of the electronic commerce, setting up physical offices is not mandatory now. Which means, even when a foreign company carries on business only through an e-commerce without a branch office in Japan, it must appoint and register its Japan representative(s).

A branch office is a part of a foreign company, and the foreign company is directly liable for the debt of the Japan branch, which may assure Japanese creditors if a foreign company has a strong financial basis and creditworthiness. On the other hand, some Japanese business partners and contractors prefer K.K. or G.K. to branch offices just because they think companies incorporated in Japan seem to show stronger commitment to the Japan markets.

When a foreign company carries out business activities through its branch office in Japan, the office is deemed as Permanent Establishment (PE). Therefore, branch offices are subject to income taxes such as corporate

11

店が獲得した利益は，通常は本国でも課税されるため二重課税が発生します。外国で納付した税金を控除することができる外国税額控除が本国で適用されることが多いと思われますが，諸外国のなかには，海外の支店が獲得した所得は免税としている国もあります。

Chapter One：事業体の選択 Business Entity

income tax, and they are required to register at the tax authority when opening the office. The profits earned by the Japan branch are usually taxed in the home country as well, resulting in double taxation. Generally, foreign tax credits — deduction of the tax amount paid in a foreign country — can be applied in the home country. Some countries exempt overseas income instead.

Q4 株式会社とはどのような会社ですか。

A 株式会社は，大規模な事業を行うことを想定した会社で，①独立した法人格，②出資者の有限責任，③出資持分の譲渡自由，④所有と経営の分離，の4つの特徴を備えた会社です。

① 独立した法人格

株式会社は，出資者（株主）から法的に独立した人格を持つため，日本子会社が獲得した債権や負担した債務は，法人格が異なる本国の本社には帰属しません。そのため，本社の債権者は，独立した法人格を有する日本の子会社の財産を債権回収のあてにすることはできません。また，日本の子会社の債権者は，人格が異なる本国本社の財産を追求することはできません。

② 出資者の有限責任

会社が支払不能に陥っても債権者は株主に請求することができないため，株主のリスクは投資元本に限定されています。なお，会社の資産しか当てにできない債権者を保護する観点から，株主が出資元本を引き上げることを認めていません。

③ 出資持分の譲渡自由

株主の投資回収の機会を確保するために，出資持分は原則として自由に譲渡できることが保証されています。ただし，プライベートカンパニーでは譲渡を制限することが認められています。

④ 所有と経営の分離

株式会社は大勢の株主が存在することを想定しています。多数の株主が直接

Chapter One : 事業体の選択 Business Entity

Q4　What is a Kabushiki Kaisha (K.K.) ?

A　Kabushiki Kaisha (K.K.) is a company designed to do a large scale of business, featuring 1) separate legal personality, 2) limited liability protection, 3) transferability of ownership, and 4) separation of ownership and management.

1) Separate legal personality

K.K. has a separate legal personality that is distinct from its investors. Which means any of the rights and obligations arising out of the transactions performed by a Japan subsidiary will not belong to its parent company in the home country. Parent company's creditors cannot rely on the assets of Japan subsidiary. Vice versa, creditors of a Japanese subsidiary are not able to chase the assets of its parent company.

2) Limited liability protection

The risk of shareholders is limited to the amount of their investment because the company's creditors cannot claim its shareholders if the company becomes insolvent. Shareholders are not allowed to withdraw their investment from the company, to protect creditors who only rely on the assets of the company.

3) Transferability of ownership

In order to secure the opportunity for shareholders to withdraw their investment, in principle, it is guaranteed that equity interests can be freely traded. However, private companies can restrict the transfers of its shares.

4) Separation of ownership and management

It is assumed that K.K. has a large number of shareholders. Since it is

会社を経営することは不可能なため，株主が選任した取締役が会社を経営します。そして，会社の役員として取締役の業務を監査する監査役，外部監査人として会社の計算書類を監査する会計監査人など，取締役を監視する仕組を置くことで株主を保護しています。株主が取締役に就任することもあるプライベートカンパニーでは，経営体制を簡素化することが可能となっています。

Chapter One：事業体の選択 Business Entity

impossible for a lot of shareholders to directly operate a company, directors appointed by shareholders will run the company.

Shareholders are protected by a monitoring system with a Corporate Auditor and an Accounting Auditor. A Corporate Auditor is a company's officer who audits the work of directors. An Accounting Auditor is an external auditor who audits the company's financial statements. Private companies, which often appoint shareholders as its directors, are allowed to make its governance structure simpler.

Q5 合同会社はどのような会社ですか。

A 合同会社は，株式会社と同様に有限責任制度を採用する一方，パートナーシップ（組合）の性格を持つ，比較的新しいタイプの法人です。合同会社は，少数の出資者が自ら会社を経営することを想定した会社で，株式会社と比べて，組織やルールについて出資者が自由に設計することができます。

　会社法は，株式会社，合名会社，合資会社，合同会社の4種類の会社を用意しています。株式会社以外の3つの会社は，出資者でありオーナーである社員が自ら経営することを想定した会社で，持分会社と呼ばれます。

　持分会社の社員には，2種類あります。会社がその財産をもってその債務を完済することができない場合には，会社の債務を弁済する責任を負う社員を無限責任社員といいます。これに対して，会社の債務に責任を負わない有限責任制度が適用される社員を有限責任社員といいます。持分会社のうち，無限責任社員だけからなる会社を合名会社，無限責任社員と有限責任社員の両方からなる持分会社を合資会社，出資者の全員が有限責任である持分会社を合同会社といいます。

　合同会社は，比較的自由に組織やルールについて設計することができます。例えば，利益の配当について，株式会社のような出資比率ではなく貢献度に応じて自由に出資者に配分することができます。資金力のある大企業と技術力をもつ中小企業が合弁事業を行う場合，出資比率が高い大企業より技術的貢献が大きい中小企業により多くの配当を行うことができます。

　このように合同会社は組合的性格をもつ会社ですが，合同会社の所得は合同会社のレベルで法人税が課税され，投資家レベルで課税されるパススルー課税の適用はありません。

18

Chapter One：事業体の選択 Business Entity

Q5 What is a Godo Kaisha (G.K.) ?

A Godo Kaisha (G.K.) is a relatively new type of business legal form that provides liability protection like K.K. and other features similar to a partnership. G.K. is designed for small businesses with a small number of investors who operate the company on their own, and it gives them more flexibility to develop its organization and internal rules.

The Companies Act provides 4 types of company, Kabushiki Kaisha (K.K.), Gomei Kaisha, Goshi Kaisha, and Godo Kaisha (G.K.). The three companies other than K.K. are membership companies, designed for members, — investors who own membership company, to operate the company on their own.

There are two types of members: one that is liable for the company's liabilities if it becomes insolvent (unlimited liability member), and one that is not liable (limited liability member). Gomei Kaisha can only have unlimited liability members while Goshi Kaisha can have both. Godo Kaisha (G.K.) is consisted of limited liability members only.

G.K. can design its organization and rules relatively freely. For example, G.K. is allowed to distribute dividends depending on how much contribution members made to the business, instead of based on the investment amount like K.K. In the case of a joint venture between a big corporation who invests more money and a SME who provides unique technology, it is possible to pay more dividends to the smaller member who made greater contribution by providing its technology.

Although G.K. features partnership characters, pass-through taxation — the income generated by a legal entity is treated as income of its owners — does not apply to G.K. Corporate income tax is imposed at the level of the entity.

19

▶▶事業体を比較検討する際のポイント

Q6　事業形態によって税金の負担は異なりますか。

A　事業形態を選択するにあたって，現地国での利益の獲得から本国への還流までのトータルの税負担がどうなるかは重要な検討項目になります。現地法人の法人税および配当の源泉所得課税のみならず，本国における課税と外国税額控除を踏まえ，トータルの税負担をシミュレーションしておく必要があります（詳細は第4章ファイナンス）。

　まず日本の税金ですが，支店，株式会社および合同会社のいずれの場合も日本で獲得した利益に対して，法人税など利益を課税標準とする税金が課せられます。実効税率は約30％です（Q84参照）。その利益を本国に送金する場合，株式会社および合同会社の配当に対して日本において20.24％の源泉税（非上場株式の場合）が課税されます。本国と日本の間に租税条約が締結され，配当に対して限界税率を定めている場合には，税率が軽減されます。支店の本店への送金は同一法人内の内部取引にすぎないため，日本で源泉税は課税されません。

　次に本国の税金ですが，本国が「全世界課税」を採用している場合には，国内所得だけでなく国外所得に対しても本国で税金が課せられます。日本支店が日本で獲得した利益は，国外所得として本国でも課税されることが一般的です。本国本社とは別法人である株式会社および合同会社に対して本国が税金を課すことは一般的にありません。配当は本国本社の国外所得となりますが，海外子会社からの配当を免税としている国は多くあります。

Chapter One：事業体の選択 Business Entity

Q6 Does the tax implication differ between types of business entity?

A When you choose a legal form for a business, it is important to know the total tax implication of the activities from earning profits in the local country to the repatriation to your home country. It is necessary to simulate the total tax burden by considering the local corporate tax and local withholding tax, as well as tax and foreign tax credit in your home country. (for details, see Chapter 4 Finance)

First of all, when you earn profits in Japan, income taxes including Corporate Tax are imposed in any case of K.K., G.K. and branch offices of foreign corporations. The effective tax rate of income taxes is approximately 30% (See Q84). When you repatriate profits to your home country, withholding tax is imposed in Japan on dividends distributed by K.K. and G.K. at the rate of 20.24% (unlisted shares). The reduced tax rate will be applied if your home country has a tax treaty with Japan which determines a reduced tax rate for dividends. Remittance from a branch office of a foreign corporation to its head office is not subject to withholding tax as it is only an internal transaction within the same legal entity.

If your home country adopts the world-wide tax system, tax is imposed on foreign sourced income at your home country as well as domestic sourced income. Profits earned by Japan branch offices are generally taxed as foreign sourced income in the home country. Profits earned by K.K. and G.K. are generally not taxed in the home country because they are separate legal entities from the head office company. Dividends from foreign subsidiaries are foreign sourced income, but many countries exempt foreign dividends from tax.

21

同じ所得に対して日本と本国の両国が課税すると二重課税が発生します。外国税額控除または国外所得免税の制度が本国にあれば，二重課税は軽減または回避することができます。

Chapter One：事業体の選択 Business Entity

Double taxation occurs when both Japan and the home country tax the same income. Double taxation can be reduced or avoided if your home country has the foreign tax deduction or the foreign income tax exemption system.

Q7 本国の親会社は日本事業から生じた債務に責任を負いますか。

A 駐在員事務所および支店は本社と切り離された法的形態ではないため，本社は日本の事業のすべての債務に対して責任を負います。株式会社および合同会社は，本国本社とは法人格が異なるため，日本の子会社の債務に対して本国の親会社は直接責任を負うことはありません。

駐在員事務所および支店は本国の外国会社の一部であり，日本の事務所のすべての債務は本社に直接帰属することから，外国会社は日本のすべての事業活動について直接責任を負っていると言えます。

一方，外国企業は日本の子会社の債務に対して責任を負いません。これは，株式会社や合同会社などの子会社は法的に外国会社から分離されているからです。そのため，外国会社が負うリスクは日本の子会社への投資額に限定されています。

ただし，合同会社の場合，出資者である外国会社は業務を執行する社員としての責任があります。社員が悪意または重過失によって第三者に損害を与えた場合には，損害を賠償する責任を直接負うことになります（会社法597条）。

なお，実務として，日本子会社が銀行から借入を行うなど親会社の信用補完が必要なときには，本社が保証を差し入れるということがあります。また，子会社の業績が悪化し，債務の弁済が困難になった場合には，レピュテーションの悪化を防ぐために，本国本社が自身の子会社に対する貸付を放棄したり，たとえ債務保証を行っていない場合でも子会社の債務を肩代わりしたりすることもあります。

Chapter One：事業体の選択 Business Entity

Q7 Is the parent company in the home country responsible for the debt of Japanese business?

A As representative offices and branch offices are not a separate legal entity from the head office company, the company is directly responsible for all the debts of operations in Japan. On the other hand, K.K. and G.K. are separate legal entities from its parent companies, and the parent companies do not directly bear the debt of its subsidiary in Japan.

Representative offices and branch offices are part of the foreign company in the home country, and all the liabilities of the Japan office directly belongs to the head office company. In other words, the foreign company is directly responsible for all the business operations in Japan.

On the other hand, a foreign company is not liable for the debts of its Japan subsidiary e.g. K.K. and G.K., which are legally separated from their foreign company. The risk to the foreign company is limited to the amount of its investment in its Japan subsidiary.

In the case of G.K., the foreign company is responsible for the role of the member who executes the operation. If a member causes damage to a third party due to bad faith or gross negligence, the member is directly liable to compensate losses arising in a third party (the Companies Act Article 597).

In practice, the parent company may provide a guarantee when a Japanese subsidiary borrows from a bank. Also, parent companies may carry out debt waiver or take over its subsidiary's debt to protect their global brand reputation when its subsidiary is experiencing financial difficulties.

25

Q8 経営者は日本に居住している必要がありますか。

A 株式会社および合同会社の役員に日本居住要件は課せられていません。外国会社の日本支店は日本における代表を定め，そのうち最低1名は日本に居住している必要があります。

　株式会社の取締役（合同会社の業務執行社員）の居住要件は2015年に緩和されました。現在は，非居住取締役（非居住業務執行社員）だけで会社を設立することが可能です。取締役の居住要件は会社法ではなく，法務省の民事局通達によって規制されています。

　以前は，代表取締役（合同会社の場合は業務執行社員）のうち少なくとも1名は日本に住所を有していないと会社を設立できませんでした。そのため，代表取締役として駐在員を日本に派遣するか，合弁相手など日本のビジネスパートナーから代表取締役を出してもらうなどの対応が必要であり，日本の居住者を代表取締役に任命できない場合には，会計事務所の職員の名義を借りるなどの対応がとられていました。

　対内直接投資を呼び込む政策の一環として，居住要件に関する規制が2015年に撤廃され，すべての取締役や業務執行社員が非居住者の場合であっても会社を設立できるようになりました。これにより，本国本社の役職員のみで取締役を構成することが可能となり，駐在員を日本に派遣しなくても日本法人の経営を本社が直接行えるようになりました。

　ただし，銀行口座の開設やオフィスの賃貸借取引において，銀行や不動産業者のなかには，代表取締役が日本に住所を有していることまたは在留資格を有することを求めるケースがあるので留意が必要です。

　これに対して，外国会社の日本支店は日本代表を定めなければならず，そのうち最低1名は日本に居住している必要があります。

Chapter One：事業体の選択 Business Entity

Q8 Does a director need to live in Japan?

A There is no directors' residency requirement for K.K. and G.K. A branch of a foreign company is required to appoint its representative(s) in Japan, at least one of which must be a resident of Japan.

Residency requirements for directors in K.K. (executive members in G.K.) were relaxed in 2015. It now allows the formation of a company with nonresident directors (executive members) alone. Directors' residency requirements are not stipulated by the Companies Act. It is regulated by circular notices issued by the Civil Affairs Bureau of the Justice Ministry.

Previously, K.K. had to have at least one representative director who had an address in Japan, otherwise the application for incorporation would be denied. Headquarters needed to dispatch an expatriate to be appointed as a representative director, or to find a resident representative director from a local business partner. Otherwise, they used nominee director services from accounting firms.

As part of the efforts to increase inward direct investment, a new circular notice was issued in March 2015 to eliminate the directors' residency requirements. It became possible to establish K.K. even if all the directors are nonresidents. You can appoint people from headquarters as directors and directly manage the Japanese K.K. without having to send expatriates to Japan.

However, when you make a deal with banks and landlords, keep in mind that some of them still follow the old policy requiring you to have a representative director who is a local resident or who has a residence permit.

On the other hand, a branch of a foreign company is required to appoint its representative(s) in Japan, and at least one of them must be a resident of Japan.

27

Q9 資本金の金額はどのように決定しますか。

A 株式会社の場合，株主が出資した金額の2分の1以上を資本金に計上し，それ以外は資本準備金として計上します。合同会社の場合，資本金に組み入れる金額は会社が自由に決定することができます。支店および駐在員事務所は外国会社の一組織であるので，支店または駐在員事務所に固有の資本金というものはなく，外国会社の資本金が参照されます。

　資本金および資本準備金（合同会社の場合は資本剰余金）は，出資元本にあたるため，両方とも配当の財源規制の対象になります。それ以外の規制においては，債権者保護規制が厳しい資本金に対し，資本準備金のほうが柔軟に利用できる場合があります。

　例えば，欠損填補において異なった取扱いがされます。過去の業績悪化により累積した赤字額を資本金および資本準備金と相殺することで，業績回復時には早期に配当を再開することが可能になります。欠損填補は配当可能額を増やすことになるため，株主にとっては好ましいことですが，債権者にとっては不利益となります。そのため，欠損填補によって資本金を相殺する場合には，債権者保護手続が必要になります。公告および催告の手続を行い，債権者が異議を申し立てた場合には，債務を弁済するまたは担保を提供する必要があります。これに対して，欠損填補で資本準備金を減少させる場合には，債権者保護手続は必要とされていません。

　そのほか，合同会社の社員が出資金の払戻しを請求する際にも，資本金を減少させる場合には債権者保護手続が必要になりますが，資本剰余金を減らす場合には不要です（Q72参照）。

Chapter One：事業体の選択 Business Entity

Q9 How is the amount of capital determined?

A K.K. is required to book at least half of the invested amount in the capital account. The rest will be booked in the capital reserve account. G.K. can freely determine the amount of capital. Branches and representative offices of a foreign company do not have its own capital as they are a part of a foreign company. The capital amount of a foreign company is referenced.

The capital and the capital reserve (capital surplus for G.K.) are invested amount from investors, and both are subject to dividend distribution regulation. In other regulations, the capital reserve can be used more flexibly while the capital is subject to strict creditor protection.

For example, the capital and the capital reserve are treated differently in disposition of deficit. By offsetting the losses accumulated over the past downturn against the capital and the capital reserve, you will be able to start to distribute dividends again as soon as the company revives its performance. Disposition of deficit is a favorable change for shareholders and a disadvantage for creditors because it increases the distributable amount. Therefore, creditor protection procedures are required if you offset against the capital. You need to carry out a public notice and notification procedures, and pay debts or provide collateral if a creditor makes an objection. On the other hand, no creditor protection procedure is required if you reduce the capital reserve to offset the deficit.

For another example, the creditor protection procedure is not required if the company refunds from capital surplus when G.K. members claim a refund of their equity while the protection is necessary if you refund from the capital (See Q72).

29

このように，債権者保護の規制において，資本金と資本剰余金に差が設けられています。資本金は，債権者が最も信頼できる基準値であり，会社の信用力を図る重要な指標となるため，登記事項として開示されます。資本金の金額は，債権者に対する信用力と，出資者の利益の両方のバランスを考えて決定すべきといえます。

　資本金額を決めるもう1つの重要なファクターは税金です。資本金が1億円以下の場合は，外形標準課税が免除されるなど多くの優遇税制が適用できます（Q10参照）。外国会社の支店の場合は，本社の資本金で優遇税制の適用が判断されるため，あえて会社を設立して資本金を引き下げることが考えられます。投資額が多い場合，2分の1を資本金に計上しなければならない株式会社に代えて，資本金額を自由に決定できる合同会社を選択する場合があります。

Chapter One：事業体の選択 Business Entity

This way, there is a distinction between the capital and the capital reserve (capital surplus) in the creditor protections. The capital is the most reliable indicator for creditors to measure up the company's credibility. The capital amount is registered in the commercial registration which is available to the public. You should take into consideration the balance between the credibility for creditors and the interests of shareholders when you determine the capital amount.

Another important consideration is tax. If the capital amount is JPY 100 million or less, you can take tax advantages for SMEs including exemption from Size-based Business Tax can be applied (See Q10). For a branch of a foreign company to take such tax advantages, the capital amount of the foreign company must be less than JPY 100 million. You may consider setting up K.K. or G.K. instead of having its Japan branch to reduce the applicable capital amount. If your investment into Japan entity is large, you may want to choose G.K. which can freely determine the capital amount.

31

Q10　資本金の額が要件となる優遇税制はありますか。

A　軽減税率を含む中小企業を支援する様々な税制上の優遇措置があります。資本金の金額は優遇措置の適用を受けるための重要な指標の１つとなっています。

資本金が1,000万円未満の場合
❏　設立初年度は消費税の免税事業者となる（Q86参照）

資本金が1,000万円以下の場合
❏　均等割で最低税額が適用される
　　均等割とは，地方税の１つで，利益の金額に関係なくすべての会社が負担する税金です。東京23区において従業者数が50人以下の会社の場合，資本金1,000万円以下であれば均等割は７万円であるのに対し，資本金が1,000万円超１億円以下の場合は18万円かかります。

資本金が１億円以下の場合
❏　外形標準課税が免除
　　外形標準課税とは，事業所の賃料や従業員の給与総額，資本金など企業規模を示す指標を課税標準とする税金です。

資本金が１億円以下の場合
　　ただし，株式または持分の100％を大法人（資本金が５億円以上である法

Chapter One：事業体の選択 Business Entity

Q10 Are there any tax advantages available for companies with a small capital amount?

A Small and medium-sized enterprises (SMEs) can use a wide range of tax advantages including the reduced tax rate. The amount of capital is one of the most important thresholds to be qualified.

If the capital is less than JPY 10 million
❑ Exemption from C-tax registration for the first year from incorporation (See Q86)

If the capital is JPY 10 million or less
❑ Per Capita Tax is minimum

Per capita tax is a local tax that all companies have to pay regardless of the amount of profits. For a company with less than 50 employees in the 23 wards of Tokyo, the tax amount will be JPY 70,000 if its capital amount is JPY 10 million or less while JPY 180,000 will be levied if the capital is more than JPY 10 million and less than JPY 100 million.

If the capital is JPY 100 million or less
❑ Exemption from Size-Based Business Tax

Size-based business tax is imposed based on the scale of the company's business such as the amount of rent payments, employee compensation, and capital amount.

If the capital is JPY 100 million or less except for companies 100% owned directly or indirectly by a large corporation (a corporation with a capital of

33

人）が直接もしくは間接に保有している場合は除きます。

❑　年800万円以下の所得に対する軽減税率

❑　特定同族会社の留保金課税の不適用（Q61参照）

❑　所得の100％まで繰越欠損金が利用可能

　　　赤字額は10年間繰り越せます。翌年以降の各事業年度の所得と相殺でき
ますが，相殺できる上限は原則として所得の50％までとされています。

❑　貸倒引当金の損金算入

❑　接待交際費が年800万円以下まで全額損金算入

資本金が１億円以下の場合

　ただし，同一の大規模法人（資本金が１億円を超える法人）に株式または持
分の２分の１以上を保有されている場合および複数の大規模法人に株式または
持分の３分の２以上を保有されている場合を除きます。

❑　少額減価償却資産の一括損金算入制度

　　　30万円未満の固定資産を一括で費用計上することが認められます（原則
は10万円未満）。

❑　中小企業投資促進税制

❑　中小企業経営強化税制

❑　研究開発税制の中小企業者特例

❑　所得拡大促進税制の中小企業者特例

Chapter One：事業体の選択 Business Entity

JPY 500 million or more).

❑ Reduced tax rate is applicable for the first JPY 8 million in Corporate Tax and Local Corporate Tax

❑ Exemption from the Retained-Earnings Tax for Specific Family Company(See Q61)

❑ Allowed to offset 100% of income against the unutilized tax loss carryforward

Losses can be carried forward over the next 10 years to utilize to offset future income. Basically, up to 50% of the current income can be offset.

❑ Allowance for doubtful accounts is tax deductible

❑ Entertainment expenses are tax deductible up to JPY 8 million

If the capital is JPY 100 million or less except for companies (A) 50% or more owned directly or indirectly by one large-scale corporation(a corporation with a capital of more than JPY 100 million) or (B) two thirds or more owned by directly or indirectly by large-scale corporations

❑ Minimum threshold for fixed asset is JPY 300,000

Assets less than JPY 300,000 can be expense at once (Basic rule is JPY100,000).

❑ SME investment promotion program

❑ SME management reinforcement program

❑ SME special treatment in R&D program

❑ SME special treatment in Income increase program

Q11 役員に対する報酬は税務上の費用となりますか。

A 租税回避行為を防止する観点から，プライベートカンパニーの役員に対する報酬は，①定期的に同額を支給する固定報酬，②期首から4カ月以内または株主総会から1カ月以内に税務当局に対して金額と支給日を事前に届け出をしたボーナスしか税務上の損金に計上できません。支店の場合，日本における代表者は，法人税法上の役員にはあたらないため，業績に連動したコミッションやボーナスはその期の損金として認められます。

　個人の配当所得に対して所得税が課税されますが，配当は法人税が課税された後の残余利益を株主に分配するため二重課税が発生します。この点，個人株主の所得税課税において二重課税を緩和する一定の控除が認められていますが，二重課税が十分に解消されているとは言えません。一方で，配当せず会社に利益を留保していると，留保金課税を受ける場合があります（Q61参照）。

　このため，個人オーナーが支配する会社では，配当ではなく自分に対する役員報酬で利益を還流しようとするインセンティブが強く働きます。決算期末の直前に役員の月額報酬を増額したり，決算賞与を支給して会社の利益をゼロに調整すれば，二重課税を完全に排除することができます。

　このような租税回避行為を防止する観点から，プライベートカンパニーの役員に対する業績に連動したコミッションやボーナスはその期の損金にすること

36

Chapter One：事業体の選択 Business Entity

Q11　Are fees for officers and directors tax deductible?

A From the viewpoint of the prevention of tax evasion behavior, remuneration for directors and other corporate officers of private companies will be tax deductible only if you pay (1) the same amount on a regular basis, (2) the bonus after you notify the amount and pay day to the tax office within 4 months after the beginning of the fiscal year or within 1 month after the annual shareholders' meeting. In the case of a branch office, commissions and bonuses linked to the performance by representatives of Japan are tax deductible because they are not corporate officers under the Corporation Tax Law.

The individual income tax will be imposed on dividends received by individual shareholders. Since dividends come from the company's after-tax earnings, double taxation will occur. Individual shareholders can take some deduction in their tax return. However, it's not enough to combat double taxation. If you retain profits within the company instead of paying dividends, the company may be subject to the retained taxation (See Q61).

Therefore, there are strong incentives for private companies to repatriate the company's profits through remuneration for the services they provide as officers and directors instead of dividends. You can completely avoid double taxation if you make the company's profits zero by increasing your monthly fees or paying performance-linked bonuses just right before the end of the fiscal year.

To prevent such tax avoidance behaviors, commissions and bonuses linked to the performance of the private company officers and directors are not permitted to be tax deductible for that period. If you want to make the

37

は認められていません。当期の業績にもとづいた賞与を損金に計上したければ，当期ではなく翌期の賞与として支給し，これを税務当局に対して事前に届け出することが考えられます。

　支店の場合，日本における代表者は，法人税法上の役員にはあたらないため，業績に応じたコミッションやボーナスはその期の損金として認められます。

Chapter One：事業体の選択 Business Entity

performance bonus deductible, you might think to pay it as bonus for the next year, instead of bonus for the current year, and notify to the tax office beforehand.

In the case of a branch office, commissions and bonuses linked to the performances by representatives of Japan are tax deductible because they are not corporate officers under the Corporation Tax Law.

Q12 日本から事業を撤退させるにはどのような方法がありますか。

A 業績不振などの理由で日本から撤退せざるを得ない場合，清算と売却の2つの撤退方法があります。事業形態によって取扱いが異なります。

① 事業を清算する

独立した法人である株式会社および合同会社を清算すると，債権者は請求する相手を失うことになるため，厳格な債務整理手続が求められます。一方，外国法人の支店の場合は，支店を閉鎖しても外国法人自体は存続するため，株式会社と比べて手続は簡易であると言えます。

株主総会の解散は特別決議によって決議します。会社の資産を公平に債権者に配当する債務整理を行う清算人の選任をし，法務局へ解散および清算人選任の登記申請を行います。清算人は，解散時の財産目録および貸借対照表を作成し，官報で会社の清算を公告し，知れたる債権者には個別に通知を行います。債権者の申立期間は最低2カ月確保する必要があります。債務を弁済した後に残余財産を株主に分配し，法務局へ清算結了の登記申請を行います。合同会社も同様の手続になります。

外国会社の支店の場合，支店の閉鎖と日本における代表者の退任の手続を行います。日本事業に関する債務が残っている場合は，引き続き外国会社が債務

Chapter One：事業体の選択 Business Entity

Q12　How do you close down your business in Japan ?

A　If you decide to withdraw your business in Japan you have two options for closure, either dissolution or selling your business. Different rules will be applied depending on the types of business entity.

① Dissolution

As a legally independent entity, K.K. and G.K. are required to take strict procedures to protect the creditors, who will no longer be able to chase payments. On the other hand, procedures for closing a branch office is relatively simple because the creditors are able to claim the head office of a foreign company after the branch closure.

Dissolution will be resolved by a special resolution at the general meeting of shareholders. The company will appoint a liquidator who will arrange a fair distribution of company's assets for the benefit of its creditors. Then, the company will register dissolution and appointment of a liquidator with the Legal Affairs Bureau. The liquidator prepares the assets list and the balance sheet at the point of dissolution, and makes an announcement on the Official Gazette that the company starts the insolvency process. Each known creditor must be informed individually. At least two months are given for the creditors to declare their outstanding claims. After distributing to the creditors, the liquidator distributes the residual assets to the shareholders, and register the completion of liquidation with the Legal Affairs Bureau. G.K. will take the same steps for the liquidation process.

In the case of a branch office, the foreign company will close the branch office and the representatives of Japan will resign. If there remained

41

を負担しますが，異議を申し出た債権者には弁済する必要があります。債権者の異議申立期間は，官報による代表者の退任公告の掲載の翌日から1カ月です。

② 事業を売却する

　株式会社の場合，保有株式を売却することで事業から撤退することができます（Q66参照）。

　合同会社も持分を譲渡することは可能ですが（Q71参照），買収側がファンドである場合など，出資者が直接会社を経営する合同会社の形態を望まないことがあります。その際は，株式会社へ組織変更してから株式を売却することが考えられます。合同会社から株式会社への変更には，債権者保護手続を行う必要があり，官報公告および個別債権者への通知が必要になります。

　支店を売却する場合，外国会社が事業を譲渡することになります。事業譲渡は，株式譲渡と異なり，保有資産や従業員の雇用契約など事業が有する資産と契約を個別に移転する必要があります。

Chapter One：事業体の選択 Business Entity

outstanding claims against the Japan branch, the foreign company will continue to be responsible. The foreign company must make immediate payments, if the creditors demand so, within one month after the announcement of the resignation of Japan representatives on the Official Gazette.

② Sell your business

In the case of K.K., you just sell out the shares (See Q66).

You can sell the equity of G.K. as well (See Q71). However, some buyers such as investment funds who do not directly operate the business may want you to transform G.K. to K.K. beforehand. Transformation requires you to undertake the creditor protection procedures, including announcement on the Official Gazette and direct notification to creditors.

If you sell your branch office, it would be an asset purchase transaction. Unlike selling shares, you need to sell each asset and transfer each contract including employment agreement.

43

PEストラクチャー
PE Structure

Q13 「PE無ければ課税無し」はどのような原則ですか。

A 自国以外の国で行ったビジネスから得た所得は，その国の固定的施設を通じて得た所得でなければ，その国では課税されないという国際課税の原則を言います。

PEとはPermanent Establishment（恒久的施設）の略称で，オフィスや工場などビジネスを行う固定的施設を指します。企業が外国でビジネスを行うと，その所得は本国で課税されるだけでなく，ビジネスを行った国でも課税されるため，二重課税が発生します。事業所得が当地国でも課税される要件を定めたものがPEです。企業が当地にPEを通じてビジネスを行っていれば当地国で課税されます。逆にいうとPEが無ければビジネスから発生した所得は課税されません。例えば，外国企業が，短期出張でまとめた商談に基づいて，日本の顧客に製品を輸出した際の売買利益は，日本の固定的施設を通じて得た利益ではないため，日本では課税されません。

Chapter Two : PEストラクチャー PE Structure

Q13　What does "No Tax Without PE" mean ?

A　It is an international principle that business profits derived in other countries are not taxed if the business is not carried on through Permanent Establishment (PE).

Permanent Establishment (PE) is defined as a fixed place through which the business of the enterprise is wholly or partly carried on, including office and factory. It would cause double taxation if enterprises do business in other countries because not only the home country but also the local country will impose tax on business profits derived from the local country. PE is a threshold to know whether your business profits performed in other countries are subject to the local taxation. If corporations create PE in other countries and do business through it, business profits are taxable in other countries. In other words, no tax will be imposed with no PE. For example, if a foreign corporation seals a deal with a Japanese customer during the short business trip to Japan, and exports their products to Japan, such business profits will not be taxed in Japan because the business is not carried on through PE.

Q14 支店はPEに該当しますか。

A 営業を行うために設置された外国法人の事業所である支店は，国内法および各租税条約でPEの1つに挙げられています。

日本の国内法はPEに該当する施設を以下のように規定しています。
- 事業の管理を行う場所，支店，事務所，工場，作業場，鉱山，石油または天然ガスの坑井，採掘場その他の天然資源を採掘する場所，その他事業を行う一定の場所（支店PE）
- 建設もしくは据付けの工事またはこれらの指揮監督の役務の提供で1年を超えて行われるもの（建設PE）
- 外国法人のために契約を締結する権限があるもの（代理人PE）

　本国が日本との間に租税条約を結んでいる場合は，租税条約が国内法に優先しますが，ほとんどの条約で支店はPEに含まれると規定しています。したがって外国法人の日本支店は日本の法人税の課税対象となります。

Chapter Two : PEストラクチャー PE Structure

Q14 Is a branch office a PE?

A As a branch is an office of a foreign corporation through which business is conducted, it is listed as a typical PE in both Japan domestic tax law and tax treaties.

Japanese domestic tax law sets out the definition of PE as follows:
- a place of management, a branch, an office, a factory, a workshop, a mine, an oil or gas well, a quarry or any other place of extraction of natural resources, and any other place to conduct business (Direct PE)
- a construction or installation project which lasts more than one year (Construction PE)
- a person who is authorized to conclude contracts on behalf of a foreign corporation (Agent PE)

If your home country has a tax treaty with Japan, the tax treaty overrides the Japanese domestic law. Most treaties list branch offices in the list of typical PEs. Therefore, a branch office of a foreign corporation is subject to the Japanese corporate income tax.

49

Q15 外国法人の施設がPEにあたらないケースはありますか。

A 活動が準備的または補助的な性格である場合には，PEから除外されます。情報収集活動など限られた活動を行っている駐在員事務所はPEには該当せず，法人税を申告する必要はありません。

　BEPSプロジェクトの最終報告を受けて平成30年3月31日に改正された国内法は，PEから除外する例外を次のように規定しています（平成31年分以後の所得税および平成31年1月1日以後に開始する事業年度分の法人税から適用開始）。

（改正前）

　次に掲げる場所は固定的施設に含まれないものとする。

1）資産を購入する業務のためにのみ使用する一定の場所

2）資産を保管するためにのみ使用する一定の場所

3）広告，宣伝，情報の提供，市場調査，基礎的研究その他その事業の遂行にとって補助的な機能を有する事業上の活動を行うためにのみ使用する一定の場所

（改正後）

　次に掲げる場所は固定的施設に含まれないものとする。ただし，事業の遂行にとって準備的または補助的な性格のものである場合に限るものとする。

1）商品の保管・展示・引渡しのためにのみ使用する一定の場所

2）商品の在庫の保管・展示・引渡しのためにのみ使用する一定の場所

3）他の者に加工させる商品を保管するためにのみ使用する一定の場所

4）商品を購入し，または，情報を収集するためにのみ使用する一定の場所

Chapter Two : PEストラクチャー PE Structure

Q15　Are there any exemptions from PE?

A　A fixed place of business will be exempted from PE if its activities are preparatory or auxiliary. A representative office which functions are limited to certain activities such as liaison will be exempted from PE and will not be subject to the Japanese corporate income tax.

Japanese tax law, which was reformed on March 31, 2018 in line with BEPS final reports, lists the exemptions as follows (The new regulation will be effective from FY 2019):

(Before)

The following places are not deemed to be PE.

1) the maintenance of a fixed place of business solely for the purpose of purchasing assets;

2) the use of facilities solely for the purpose of storage of assets;

3) the maintenance of a fixed place of business solely for the purpose of carrying out advertisement, collecting information, market research, fundamental research and development, or any other activity of a preparatory or an auxiliary character

(After)

The following places are not deemed to be PE, provided that such activity is of a preparatory or an auxiliary character.

1) the use of facilities solely for the purpose of storage, display or delivery of goods or merchandise belonging to the enterprise;

2) the maintenance of a stock of goods or merchandise belonging to the enterprise solely for the purpose of storage, display or delivery;

51

5）その他準備的または補助的な活動

6）上記の組合せ

BEPS（Base Erosion and Profit Shifting（税源浸食と利益移転））プロジェクトとは，一部の多国籍企業による，各国の税制の違いや抜け穴を利用した課税逃れに対し，各国税制の調和を通じて対応するためにOECDによって平成24年6月に立ち上げられたプロジェクトです。

従来の規定では，倉庫業務のみを行う施設はPEには該当しないとされていたため，日本に倉庫を置いて諸外国でインターネット販売するビジネスには課税されない可能性がありました。改正によって，そのような特定活動であっても，準備的または補助的な性格である場合に限りPEから除外する規定に変更されました。

国内法に優先する租税条約も今後改正されていく見込みですが，世界全体で1,100以上に上る租税条約を個別に改正することは非常に負担となることから，同時に改正を図るための枠組として，多国間条約である「BEPS防止措置実施条約」が導入され，日本を含む87カ国・地域が参加していますが（2019年4月1日現在），適用される規定および適用の開始は各締約国の選択に応じて異なります。ただし，米国など多国間条約に参加していない国もあります。

Chapter Two : PEストラクチャー PE Structure

3) the maintenance of a stock of goods or merchandise belonging to the enterprise solely for the purpose of processing by another enterprise;

4) the maintenance of a fixed place of business solely for the purpose of purchasing goods or merchandise or of collecting information, for the enterprise;

5) the maintenance of a fixed place of business solely for the purpose of carrying on, for the enterprise, any other activity of a preparatory or auxiliary character;

6) the maintenance of a fixed place of business solely for any combination of activities mentioned in subparagraphs

Base erosion and profit shifting (BEPS) Project is a project launched in June 2012 by OECD to develop standards to prevent tax avoidance strategies that exploit gaps and mismatches in tax rules, with over 100 countries and jurisdictions collaborating to implement the BEPS measures and tackle BEPS.

Previously, a fixed place which function is limited to warehouse operation was exempted from PE. The Japanese income tax might have not been imposed on businesses which conduct sales activities outside of Japan through the internet and deliver to Japanese customers through its warehouse located in Japan. With the reformed tax law, the exclusion can only be applied to certain activities which are regarded as of preparatory or auxiliary nature.

Tax treaties, which override the domestic tax law, are expected to be revised. To reduce time spent in negotiating bilateral, "Multilateral Convention to Implement Tax Treaty Related Measures to Prevent Base Erosion and Profit Shifting"("Multilateral Instrument" or "MLI") was introduced. 87 jurisdictions including Japan have joined (April 1, 2019). The applicable provisions and the start of application will depend on the choice of each country. Some countries including the United States have not participated in the MLI.

53

日米租税条約は，例外について次のように規定しています。

次に掲げる場所は固定的施設に含まれないものとする。

A. 商品の保管・展示・引渡しのためにのみ使用する一定の場所

B. 商品の在庫の保管・展示・引渡しのためにのみ使用する一定の場所

C. 他の者に加工させる商品を保管するためにのみ使用する一定の場所

D. 商品を購入し，または，情報を収集するためにのみ使用する一定の場所

E. その他準備的または補助的な活動

F. 上記の組合せ

　現在の日米租税条約では，AまたはBの規定によって倉庫業務はPEから除外される可能性があります。この点，OECDのモデル条約の解釈指針であるOECDコメンタリーでは，「これらの例外規定は準備的または補助的な性格の活動の例示である」と解説していますが，その解釈をめぐっては国際的にも見解が対立しています。日本では，恒久的施設該当性が訴訟上正面から争点とされる例は極めて少ないなか，例外規定は「準備的または補助的な性格の活動」の例示であると文理上解することができるとして，日本に倉庫を持つ国外のインターネット販売事業者に対する日本の課税当局の課税を認めた判例（上告申係属中）がある点は留意が必要です（東京高判平成28年1月28日・裁判所ウェブサイト）。

Chapter Two : PEストラクチャー PE Structure

Tax treaty between Japan and the US describes the exemptions:

Notwithstanding the preceding provisions of this Article, the term "permanent establishment" shall be deemed not to include:

A. the use of facilities solely for the purpose of storage, display or delivery of goods or merchandise belonging to the enterprise;

B. the maintenance of a stock of goods or merchandise belonging to the enterprise solely for the purpose of storage, display or delivery;

C. the maintenance of a stock of goods or merchandise belonging to the enterprise solely for the purpose of processing by another enterprise;

D. the maintenance of a fixed place of business   solely for the purpose of purchasing goods or merchandise or of collecting information, for the enterprise;

E. the maintenance of a fixed place of business solely for the purpose of carrying on, for the enterprise, any other activity of a preparatory or auxiliary character;

F. the maintenance of a fixed place of business solely for any combination of activities mentioned in subparagraphs (a) to (e), provided   that the overall activity of the fixed place of business resulting from this combination is of a preparatory or an auxiliary character.

Under the current treaty, warehouses might be judged as exempted from PE according to A or B. Although OECD COMMENTARIES ON THE ARTICLES OF THE MODEL TAX CONVENTION states "The common feature of these activities is that they are, in general, preparatory or auxiliary activities," there have been arguments about the interpretation around the world. In Japan, among extremely few cases dealing PE issues, Tokyo High Court made an important judgement on January 28, 2016. The court judged that the list of exceptions in the treaty are illustrative enumeration of preparatory or auxiliary activities, in favor of the tax authority which had imposed the Japanese income tax on the overseas internet merchandise with a warehouse in Japan.

55

Q16 日本で課税される支店の利益はどのように算定しますか。

A 支店が本店から分離・独立した企業であるとみなし，支店と本店との間の内部取引に独立企業間価格を適用して算定した利益に対して課税されます。

　本店から商品を輸入し日本の顧客に販売している場合，支店の仕入価格は独立企業間価格，すなわち独立した輸入業者であったならば販売していたであろう価格を，内部取引の価格に採用する必要があります。

　支店の機能が限定されている場合，例えば本店のために新規顧客開拓だけを行っている場合には，支店から本店に対してサービスを提供しているとみなし，独立企業間価格に基づいたサービス収益を計上します。

　支店と本店の取引は同一法人内の内部取引であるため，契約を締結することは通常ありませんが，税法は内部取引について文書化を義務づけています。したがって，この内部取引が独立企業間価格に基づいていることを立証できるよう内部の合意書など取引証憑をそろえておく必要があります。

Chapter Two : PEストラクチャー PE Structure

Q16 How are the profits of the branch measured?

A A branch is regarded as a separate and independent company from the head office. The arm's length price is applied to the internal transactions between the branch and the head office.

If a branch imports the goods from the head office and sells to Japanese customers, the internal purchase price should be an arm's length price, a price that would be applied if the branch were a separate and independent importer.

If the function of a branch is limited to certain activities such as business marketing to find new leads for the head office, it is deemed that the services are rendered from the branch to its head office at the price of arm's length.

Since the deals made between a branch and its head office are merely internal transactions within the same legal entity, contracts are usually not made. However, supporting documents are required to be kept by the tax law as evidence to prove the price is arm's length. In this regard, documents such as internal agreement should be prepared to prove that the internal transactions are carried on at the arm's length price.

Q17　子会社はPEに該当しますか。

A　株式会社や合同会社など本国本社から独立した法人は，たとえ本国本社に株式保有を通じて支配されているとしても，それだけで本国本社の恒久的施設には認定されません。ただし，従属代理人として本社のビジネスに関与している場合には代理人PE認定を受け（Q14参照），本社の日本における事業所得が日本で課税されます。

　日本に支店を設置するかわりに，代理人に本人の名義で事業を行わせると，PE課税を回避しつつ，日本に支店を設けた場合と同じように事業を行うことができます。そのような行為を防止するために，本人の支配が及ぶ代理人（従属代理人）は本人のPEとして認定されます。例えば，日本の子会社が外国親会社の代理人となり，日本の顧客に対して継続的に注文をとり，外国親会社が顧客に直接輸出販売している場合，日本の子会社は外国親会社の従属代理人としてPE判定され，外国親会社の商品販売利益は日本で課税されます。

　一方で，仲立人，問屋その他の独立の地位を有する代理人が，通常の事業として外国企業の日本でのビジネスを仲介しているのであれば，それら代理人は当該外国企業のPEと判定されることはありません。

Chapter Two：PEストラクチャー PE Structure

$\mathrm{Q}17$ **Can a subsidiary create a PE?**

A Independent entities that are legally separated from the head office such as Kabushiki Kaisha and Godo Kaisha are not deemed a PE just because it is controlled through shareholding. If a subsidiary is engaged in the business of the parent company as a dependent agent, the subsidiary is deemed to be an Agent PE (See $\mathrm{Q}14$) of the parent, and the profits that the parent company earned in Japan will be taxed in Japan.

If a foreign enterprise, instead of setting its branch, has an agent in Japan who conducts a business in the name of the foreign enterprise, it is able to avoid PE taxation and do the same business as if it established its branch. To prevent such tax avoidance, "dependable agent", an agent who is controlled by an enterprise, is deemed to be a PE of the enterprise. In the case that a Japanese subsidiary is appointed as an agent of the foreign parent company, and the subsidiary constantly takes the orders from local customers, and the parent exported goods directly to the customers, the subsidiary is deemed as a PE of the parent company. The profits that the parent earned in the business of export is taxable in Japan.

On the other hand, a foreign enterprise is not deemed to have a PE, if it carries on business in Japan through a broker, general commission agent or any other agent of an independent status, provided that such people are acting in the ordinary course of their business.

59

Q18 コミッショネア方式で親会社の商品を売買していますがPE に該当しますか。

A BEPSの最終報告を受けた改正により日本国内法では，子会社がコミッショネア契約に基づいて販売している場合，外国親会社のPEとして認定されることになりました。

　通常の代理取引では，代理人は委託者の名義で取引を行い，代理人は代理手数料をもらいます。これに対して，代理人が自らの名義で販売を行いつつ，取引による損益は委託者に帰属させ，代理人は手数料をもらう取引をコミッショネア取引といいます。コミッショネア取引は，日本の商法でいう問屋取引（商法551条）に該当します。

　世界のほとんどの租税条約では，OECDモデル条約にならって，代理人PEを「外国企業の名において契約を締結する権限を有する（has an authority to conclude contracts in the name of the enterprise)」場合に限定していました。そのため，代理人が自己の名で販売するコミッショネア契約では，外国企業はPEの認定を受けることなく商品を販売することができました。通常の販売取引で得られる利益と比べて，在庫リスクを負わないコミッショネア取引における問屋が得るコミッションフィーは低いことから，PEリスクを回避しつつ，現地国における課税所得を圧縮することが可能になります。そのため，多国籍企業のなかには，現地子会社の機能を大きく変えないまま，子会社との契約を通常の仕入取引からコミッショネア取引に変更した例があったといわれています。

　OECDのモデル条約の解釈指針であるOECDコメンタリーでは，「取引の名義が文字通り外国企業である場合には限られない」と解説していましたが，そ

60

Chapter Two：PEストラクチャー PE Structure

Q18 If a subsidiary is selling products purchased from its foreign parent company under the contract of commissionaire, is the subsidiary deemed as a PE?

A Under the new domestic tax law reformed in line with the BEPS final report, a foreign enterprise is deemed to have a PE if its subsidiary is dealing under the contract of the commissionaire.

Under a normal agent agreement, the agent concludes contracts in the name of the principal, and receives agent fee. Under a commissionaire agreement, the agent sells products "in its own name" while profits belong to the principal and the agent receives agent fee. The commissionaire falls under "Commission merchant's transactions" stipulated in the Japanese Commercial Code (Code 551).

Most tax treaties in the world, which had been negotiated based on the OECD Model Convention, defined a dependent agent as a person which "has an authority to conclude contracts in the name of the enterprise." Through a commissionaire arrangement where an agent is selling "in its own name," a foreign enterprise was technically able to sell its products without having a permanent establishment. Since an agent bears no inventory risk and agent fee is smaller than normal buy & sell transactions, foreign enterprises can reduce tax in other countries without PE risk. It is said that some multinational enterprises changed the transaction agreement with its foreign subsidiaries from the normal purchase agreement to the commissionaire arrangement, without material changes in the functions performed by their local subsidiaries.

Although the previous OECD COMMENTARIES ON THE ARTICLES OF THE MODEL TAX CONVENTION stated the phrase "authority to conclude

61

の解釈をめぐっては国際的にも見解が対立していました。OECD諸国において、コミッショネアを争点とする税務訴訟が数多く提訴され、法廷で争われたケースの大半において、課税当局の主張は退けられていました。

　BEPSプロジェクトにおいてコミッショネア問題は最重要の論点の1つとして議論され、2015年10月に出された最終報告書において、コミッショネア方式をPE認定することを提案しました。これを受けて、日本の国内法は、平成30年度の税制改正で、販売者の名義の如何にかかわらず、外国企業の資産の所有権の移転に関する契約を扱う従属代理人であればPEとして認定されることになりました。国内法に優先する租税条約は、多国間条約による改定を目指しています（Q15参照）。

Chapter Two : PEストラクチャー PE Structure

contracts in the name of the enterprise" does not confine the application of the paragraph to an agent who enters into contracts literally in the name of the enterprise," there were arguments about the interpretation around the world. Numerous cases dealing with commissionaire arrangement were litigated in OECD countries. In most of the cases that went to court, the tax administration's arguments were rejected.

The BEPS Project discussed the commissionaire as one of the most important issues to be addressed, and proposed in its final report issued in October 2015 that a commissionaire should be deemed as a PE. To respond to the final report, the Japanese tax law was reformed in 2018. Under the new law, a dependent agent dealing with products owned by a controlling foreign enterprise is to be deemed a PE, regardless of the name of the seller. Tax treaties, which override the domestic tax law, are expected to be revised through MLI(See Q15).

Q19　コストプラスカンパニーとはどのような会社ですか。

A　現地の顧客に商品およびサービスを輸出する外国関係会社に対して，サポートサービスを提供する現地会社のことをコストプラスカンパニーと呼びます。

十分なリソースが日本の子会社にないことから，商品やサービスは外国親会社が顧客に提供し，子会社の機能を市場調査，新規顧客開拓，カスタマーサポートなど事業の一部分に限定することがあります。その場合，子会社から親会社に対してサービスを提供する契約を結び，日本の活動で生じたコストにマークアップしたサービスフィーを請求するのが一般的です。そのような形態の会社をコストプラスカンパニーと呼びます。

コストプラス方式の子会社が販売活動にかかわってくると，外国親会社のPEに認定されるリスクがあるので注意が必要です。子会社が日本の顧客に対して継続的に注文をとり，外国親会社が顧客に直接輸出販売をしている場合，日本の子会社は外国親会社の代理人としてPE判定され，外国親会社の商品販売利益が日本で課税されます（Q17参照）。

日本の子会社が販売活動や在庫管理を始めるには，コストプラス契約から子会社が商品を購入し顧客に販売する購買契約に切り替える必要があります。その場合，在庫リスクを負わないコミッショネア方式を採用して，仕入価格を高めに設定し日本での課税所得を圧縮しようとすると，PE認定されるリスクがあるので注意が必要です（Q18参照）。

64

Chapter Two：PEストラクチャー PE Structure

Q19　What's a cost-plus company?

A　A cost-plus company is a local company which provides support services to its foreign affiliate company that exports the goods and services to local customers.

Due to insufficient resources in the newly set-up Japanese subsidiary, some foreign enterprises continue to sell its goods and services directly to Japanese customers, and the Japanese subsidiary provides support services such as market research, business development, and customer support for the parent company. A service agreement will be made with the parent company, which will determine the service fees by marking up the costs that the Japanese subsidiary has spent on its activities. This type of company is called a "cost-plus company."

If a cost-plus company gets involved in sales activities, it gives rise to the PE taxation risk. For instance, if the subsidiary is involved in ordering process, repeatedly taking orders from local customers for its parent to sell the goods directly to the customers, the subsidiary will be deemed as a dependent agent and the sales profits of the parent will be taxed in Japan (See Q17).

If the Japanese subsidiary starts to conduct sales activities and inventory administrations, it should shift from cost-plus service agreement to a purchase agreement where the subsidiary purchases the products from its parent to sell to local customers. If you choose the commissionaire method to release the subsidiary from the inventory risk and determine the purchase price at a lower rate than a normal purchase agreement, it may cause PE risk (See Q18).

65

Q20 外国親会社から日本の子会社が商品を輸入する際，仕入値はどのように決定すれば良いですか。

A 法人税の計算においては，独立した第三者間において同種の取引が行われた場合に成立すると認められる価格，すなわち独立企業間価格が適用されます。したがって，同一企業グループの内部取引であっても，経済的に合理的な説明が可能な価格を設定しておく必要があります。

　企業グループ内部の取引価格は，税金を減らす目的で恣意的に決定される可能性があります。税金が高い国の会社の仕入値を相場より高めに設定することで，利益を税率の低い国へ移転させ，グループ全体の法人税を減らすことができます。このような操作を防止する税制が移転価格税制です。資本や人的に支配関係にある外国会社との取引は，独立企業間価格で行われたものとして課税所得金額を再計算する権限が課税当局に与えられています。したがって，税務調査においてそのような指摘を受けることがないよう，取引価格が独立企業間価格となっていることが説明できるよう準備しておくことが大切です。

Chapter Two : PEストラクチャー PE Structure

Q20 How do you determine the purchase price when a subsidiary imports the goods from its foreign parent?

A Arm's length price, a price that would be determined on the same transaction with an independent third party, is applied at the calculation of the corporate income tax. Therefore, it is necessary to set a price that is economically reasonable even for internal transactions of the same business group.

Pricing on the international transactions within the same enterprise group is likely to be determined deliberately in order to reduce tax amounts. If the purchase price is determined higher than the market price when the buyer's country has a higher tax rate than the seller's, profits are shifted to the tax-lower country, and the total tax amounts of the group is reduced. To prevent such tax avoidance, transfer pricing has been established, which gives tax authorities the right to recalculate the income of an enterprise by applying an arm's length price to the transactions with foreign affiliate corporations. It is important to be prepared to explain that the price of the transaction is the arm's length price so that tax officers will be satisfied during their tax audits.

Chapter

3

コーポレートガバナンス
Corporate Governance

▶▶コーポレートガバナンスとは

Q21 コーポレートガバナンスとは何ですか。

A 経営者による不正を防止するために，経営者の経営を規律し監視する組織としての仕組を一般的にコーポレートガバナンス（企業統治）といいます。

事業を行うためには，事業戦略を決定し，経営資源を投入し，製品やサービスを販売し，雇用した従業員を管理しなければなりません。もし，出資者自らが事業を運営できない場合には，経営のプロに経営を委任します。特に上場している株式会社は，大多数の投資家から資金を集めて事業を行っており，大勢の株主が自ら会社を経営することは不可能でしょう。経営を委任する場合，依頼者（出資者）の利益に反して代理人（経営者）自身の利益を優先した行動をとってしまういわゆる「エージェント問題」が常に生じます。

例えば，従業員の給与を決定する権限をもつ経営者が，自分の報酬をも決定できるとなると，過大な報酬を受け取る可能性があります。また，重要な機密情報にアクセスできる経営者が，企業のノウハウや顧客リストを流用して企業と同じ事業を始めてしまう可能性があります。

このような経営者による不正を防止するために，経営者の経営を規律し監視する仕組が必要になります。このような仕組を一般的にコーポレートガバナンス（企業統治）といいます。

Chapter Three : コーポレートガバナンス Corporate Governance

Q21 What is corporate governance?

A Corporate governance is a system of an organization that regulates and oversees the management to prevent management fraud.

During the course of business, you determine a business strategy, input resources, sell the products, and manage human resources. If the owner of the business is not able to manage the business, the management is delegated to professional managers. Especially for listed companies that are funded by a number of shareholders, it is almost impossible for a lot of shareholders to directly conduct the business. When delegating management, the principal-agent problem always occurs. The agent (manager) is motivated to act in his or her own best interests, which may be contrary to those of their principals (investors).

For instance, if the management who have the power to determine the employees' salary level are also able to decide their own fee, they may receive the fee that is more than they deserve. There is a possibility that the management who can access to the classified information may want to use the know-how and client lists to start the same business by themselves.

To prevent managers from misconducting, it is necessary to build up a system to govern and monitor the management. Such a system is generally called corporate governance.

71

Q22　コーポレートガバナンスは事業形態によってどのように異なりますか。

A　出資者と経営者が分離した株式会社に対して，会社法は株主の利益を保護する規定を数多く置いています。出資者が自ら経営にあたる合同会社では比較的自由にコーポレートガバナンスを設計できます。外国会社の一営業所である支店の統治について日本の会社法による規制はありません。

株式会社は，大多数の投資家から資金を集め，経営のプロである取締役に経営を委任することを想定した会社です。そのため，会社法は，経営者を監視して多数の株主の利益を保護する規定を数多く置いています。ただし，株主の人数が少ない中小企業も株式会社の制度を利用できるよう，より簡素なコーポレートガバナンスを選択することができます。会社法は，大企業向けである「取締役会設置会社」と，中小企業のために組織を簡素化した「取締役会非設置会社」の2つのタイプの株式会社を定めて，コーポレートガバナンスについて異なるルールを適用しています。

一方，合同会社は，出資者が自ら事業を行うことを想定した会社です。出資者であり経営者でもある社員が，その個性を生かして事業を経営します。エージェント問題が生じない合同会社のコーポレートガバナンスは，当事者の合意によって，より自由に設計することができるようになっています。例えば，社員の議決権は原則として1人1議決権ですが，定款によって特定の社員にすべての決定権を委ねることも可能です。

これに対して，支店は外国会社の一営業所であるため，支店の統治の在り方について日本の会社法は規定していません。

Chapter Three : コーポレートガバナンス Corporate Governance

Q22 How does corporate governance vary between business entities?

A The Companies Act lays down a number of clauses to protect the interests of shareholders of K.K. which investors and management are separated. G.K., whose investors conduct the management on their own, can design its corporate governance more freely. A branch of a foreign corporation is not governed by the Companies Act.

K.K. is a company which is designed to raise funds widely from a lot of investors and delegate the management to directors, professional managers. The Companies Act set forth a number of clauses to establish a monitoring mechanism to protect shareholders' interests. Small and medium-size enterprises with a small number of shareholders can choose a simple type of corporate governance. The Companies Act defines two types of K.K., "Company with Board of Directors" for large corporations and "Company without Board of Directors" which is designed for SMEs, applying different rules for corporate governance.

G.K. is a company which is designed for investors to execute a business by themselves. Investors who are also managers run a business, making use of their originality. Corporate governance of G.K., which does not have agent problems, can be designed more flexibly with the investors' agreement. For example, despite the general rule which gives one voting right to each member, it is possible to delegate all decisions to a certain member by stating so in the articles of incorporation.

Corporate governance of a branch office is not governed by the Japanese Companies Act because it is an office of a foreign corporation.

73

Q23 日本の事業に対してどのようなコーポレートガバナンスを構築すべきですか。

A 日本の経営陣を本国の本社から監視する体制を構築すべきです。

　本国から時差があり物理的に離れた海外拠点では，必然的に本国本社の監視の目は届きにくくなるため，現地の経営者による不正が発生する可能性は高いと言えます。そのため，本国の役職員を非居住取締役に選任して取締役の過半数を押さえる，外部の監査法人による会計監査を導入する，本国から定期的に内部監査チームを派遣するなどの監視体制を構築することが大切です。

　経営者候補として，まず，本国の本社の従業員を日本に出向派遣して経営にあたらせることが考えられます。本社から見ると，駐在員は同僚であるため，忠誠心が高く会社を裏切ることはないと考え，経営者を監視する仕組であるコーポレートガバナンスの構築をおろそかにしがちです。しかしながら，駐在員を信頼し経営を任せきりにしてしまうと，例えば取引先と結託してキックバックを受領するなど，不正が発生するリスクが高まるため注意が必要です。

　企業によっては，日本のマーケットや慣習に習熟しているローカル人材に経営を任せたほうが成長が早いという判断から，進出当初から日本人または日本に居住している同胞者を雇い入れて経営にあたらせる場合があります。外部の経営者を採用することになるので，一定の警戒感のもとに経営者の監視体制を構築する傾向が見られます。

Chapter Three : コーポレートガバナンス Corporate Governance

Q23 What kind of corporate governance should be established for the operation in Japan?

A It is important to establish an effective system that enables the headquarters to monitor the local management in Japan.

Overseas operations are at a higher risk of local management fraud as it is difficult to monitor the place far from the home country with time lag. To tackle this issue, it is essential to establish an effective monitoring system, appointing non-resident directors from the head office to obtain the majority of voting, engaging local external auditors, and periodically sending internal audit team from the head office.

You may want to send a loyal employee from the head office to manage the new operation. Since expatriates are colleagues, the head office tends to think they are highly loyal and never betray the company, neglecting to put them under a robust monitoring system. However, trust is not an internal control. Too much trust undermines the monitoring system, causing incidents such as kick back transactions by the local management colluding with local suppliers.

On the other hand, some foreign corporations hire local talents to appoint as directors when they start business in Japan with hope that the local people with the best knowledge about the local market will drive the business performance more. With external people joining the local management, the head offices tend to develop an efficient monitoring system with caution.

75

▶▶株式会社のコーポレートガバナンス
▶コーポレートガバナンスの類型

Q24 「取締役会設置会社」とはどのような会社ですか。

A 「取締役会設置会社」とは，正式な会社の機関として取締役会を設ける株式会社です。しっかりとしたコーポレートガバナンスの仕組を備えており，上場企業，ベンチャーキャピタルが投資したスタートアップ，日本法人の取締役の監視を強化したい外資系企業などに適した形態であるといえます。

　チェックアンドバランスを向上させ，コーポレートガバナンスに規律を与えるために，会社の権限は2つの機関，取締役会と代表取締役に分けられます。取締役会が決定を下し，代表取締役が執行者としてこれを実行します。

　取締役会は3人以上の取締役の全員で構成しなければならず，合議によって業務に関する意思決定を行います。意思決定の権限の一部を代表取締役に委譲することができますが，「多額の借財」を行う場合（会社法362条4項2号）など，意思決定を委譲することができない事項が法律で定められています。

　会社の別の機関として事業を執行する代表取締役は，取締役会の投票により取締役のなかから選任され，取締役会が決定した業務を執行します。代表取締役以外の取締役は，取締役会の決議による委任または代表取締役からの委任によって業務を執行することができます。業務を執行する取締役を「業務執行取締役」といいます。業務執行取締役のうち，代表取締役は代表権を有しています。代表権とは，特段の手続を得ることなく単独で会社を代理することができる権限です。取引の相手方にとっては，代表取締役が行った対外的行為は会社に帰属するため，権限が委任されていることを個別に確かめる必要がなく，取引を保護する機能を有しています。

Chapter Three：コーポレートガバナンス Corporate Governance

Q24　What is a "Company with Board of Directors" ?

A　A "Company with Board of Directors" is a type of Kabushiki Kaisha which has a board of directors as an official governance body. As Company with Board of Directors can build a robust corporate governance, it is preferred by public companies, startups invested by venture capital, and subsidiaries of foreign corporations who wish to establish a strong monitoring system on local directors.

In order to increase checks and balances and give corporate governance integrity, powers of the company are separated into two branches; a board of directors and a representative director. A board of directors makes the decisions and a representative director carries them out as the executive.

A board of directors which consists of at least three directors makes decisions by voting after discussions and debates. Some decision-making powers can be delegated to a representative director to the extent that the Companies Act allows. Important decisions such as borrowing in a significant amount are not allowed to be made by representative directors (the Companies Act Article 362(4)(ii)).

A representative director, another branch of the company which executes the business, is elected among directors by votes of a board of directors. Representative directors execute the decisions made by the board of directors. Other directors may have executive powers if they are delegated by the board of directors or representative directors. Directors who execute operations are called "executive directors". Among executive directors, a representative director has the power of a representative, which is the power to have the authority to sign on behalf of the company without any delegation procedures. Counterparties who make a deal with a

77

代表取締役を選任する権限をもち，業務執行取締役の業務執行をモニタリングする取締役会は，監査役によりモニタリングされます。監査役とは，会社の機関の1つで，株主の利益のために取締役を監視します。日本独特のダブルモニタリングシステムである監査役は，英語ではCorporate AuditorまたはAudit & Supervisory Board Memberと訳されています（Q47参照）。監査役の設置に代えて，他の「監査等委員会設置会社」または「指名委員会等設置会社」という他の2つのモニタリングシステムを選ぶこともできます。

　取締役会を中心とした経営組織が整備されている取締役会設置会社では，経営の大部分を取締役に委任できるため，株主総会の決議事項は法令・定款で定めた事項に限定されています。

Chapter Three : コーポレートガバナンス Corporate Governance

representative director do not have to check if the representative director has the authority to do so.

A board which has the power to appoint representative directors and monitor executive directors is monitored by a Kansayaku, an officer of the company whose roll is observing directors to protect shareholders' interests. Kansayaku is a double monitoring system unique to Japan, which can be translated as "Corporate Auditor" or "Audit & Supervisory Board Member" (See Q47). Instead of appointing Kansayaku, the company can choose from two other options for its monitoring system, "Company with audit committee" and "Company with nominating committee".

As Company with Board of Directors delegates most parts of management to directors, powers of shareholders' meeting are limited to the extent that the Companies Act and the articles of incorporation allow.

Q25 「取締役会非設置会社」とはどのような会社ですか。

A 「取締役会非設置会社」とは，会社の機関としての取締役会を設置しない株式会社です。簡素なコーポレートガバナンスを構築することができるため，中小企業に向いた形態です。

取締役会非設置会社は，取締役は1名以上であればよく，各取締役は単独で業務に関する意思決定と業務の執行を行います。支店の設置など一部の重要事項に限り取締役の過半数で決定します。

すべての取締役が代表取締役となります。すなわち，会社を代表して第三者と取引を締結する権限をもちます。特定の取締役だけに代表権を与えることも可能です。

取締役会非設置会社の株主総会は，株式会社に関する一切の事項について決議することが可能なため，株式会社の経営に深く関与することができます。そのため，取締役会非設置会社は必ずしも取締役を監視する監査役（Q47参照）を置く必要はありません。

このように，業務に関する意思決定と業務執行の在り方について比較的自由に設計できる取締役会非設置会社は，比較的少数の株主と取締役が信頼関係で結ばれており，取締役同士も緊密に連携しているような中小企業に向いているといえます。

Chapter Three：コーポレートガバナンス Corporate Governance

Q25　What is a "Company without Board of Directors" ?

A　A "Company without Board of Directors" is a type of Kabushiki Kaisha which does not have a board of directors as an official government body. As a Company without Board of Directors can build simple corporate governance, it is often chosen by small and medium-sized enterprises.

A Company without Board of Directors can be formed with at least one director. Each director has the power of both decision-making and execution. A few important matters such as establishing a branch office require a majority of the votes of directors.

Every director is a representative director which has the authority to sign on behalf of the company without any delegation procedures. The power of representative can be given only to certain directors.

The shareholders' meeting is able to decide everything so that the shareholders are involved deeply in the company's management. This is the reason Corporate Auditors (See Q47), an officer whose role is to monitor directors for shareholders, are not necessarily appointed by a Company without Board of Directors.

This way, a Company without Board of Directors can design how to decide and execute the business more freely. It is often chosen by small and medium-size enterprises with a few shareholders well connected to directors who are working closely with each other.

81

Q26 「株式譲渡制限会社」とはどのような会社ですか。

A 「株式譲渡制限会社」とは，発行するすべての株式について，譲渡する場合に会社の承認を得る必要がある会社をいいます。

　株式会社は，株式の譲渡は自由に行えることが原則です（Q4参照）。しかしながら，上場企業以外の会社では，株式が自由に売買されることで見知らぬものが株主となって経営に入ってくることを好みません。そこで，株式を譲渡する場合には会社の承認を必要とする譲渡制限を設けることが認められています。「株式譲渡制限会社」において株式の譲渡を承認するのは，「取締役会設置会社」では取締役会，「取締役会非設置会社」では株主総会（定款により代表取締役とすることも可）です。

　すべての株式に譲渡制限を課した会社を「株式譲渡制限会社（プライベートカンパニー）」と呼び，それ以外の会社を「公開会社（パブリックカンパニー）」といいます。

　株主が多数存在しうる「公開会社」には「株式譲渡制限会社」と比べてより高度なガバナンスが求められます。例えば，公開会社は取締役会を必ず設置しなければならず，取締役の任期は2年より伸長することはできません。一方で，公開会社は株式市場から機動的な資金調達を可能にするため，株主総会ではなく取締役会の決議で株式を発行することができます。

　株式会社の重要な機能を選択するにあたり，以下の3パターンがあります。

	取締役会設置会社	取締役会非設置会社
公開会社	パターン1	―
株式譲渡制限会社	パターン2	パターン3

Chapter Three : コーポレートガバナンス Corporate Governance

Q26 What is a "Private Company" ?

A A "Private Company" is a type of Kabushiki Kaisha with all shares restricted to be sold without permission from the company.

One of the important principles in Kabushiki Kaisha is that the shareholders have the right to sell shares freely (See Q4). However, companies other than listed companies do not want strangers to become shareholders and be involved in the management. The Companies Act allows Kabushiki Kaisha to place a restriction on transferring its shares. The shareholders are required to ask for an approval from the company when they sell shares of the company, and the board gives permission. In the case of Company without Board of Directors, shareholders' meeting gives permission unless the articles of incorporation describe that representative directors do.

A K.K. which puts restrictions on all the shares is called a "Private Company", and the rest is called "Public Company". As a Public Company has numerous shareholders, a stronger governance is required by the Companies Act. For example, a Public Company must be a Company with Board of Directors, and the director's 2-year term cannot be extended. On the other hand, a Public Company can issue new shares with the resolution of the board of directors in order to raise funds quickly at the market, while a Private Company is required to get permission from the shareholders' meeting.

There are three patterns when you choose the major features of K.K.

	Company with Board of Directors	Company without Board of Directors
Public Company	Pattern 1	—
Private Company	Pattern 2	Pattern 3

83

▶*株主および株主総会*

Q27 株主にはどのような権利が与えられ，どのような義務および責任を負っていますか。

A 株主には，会社から経済的利益を受ける権利（自益権）と，会社の経営を支配する権利（共益権）が与えられています。これに対して，株主は会社に対して義務は負っていません。

利益の配当を受ける権利は自益権を代表する権利です。最も重要な共益権は，株主総会の議決権です。多数の出資者を想定する株式会社では，株主が直接経営を行うことが予定されていないため，株主総会という会議体で多数決によって取締役の選任など重要な事項を決定し，実際の経営は経営のプロである取締役が執行することになります。

投資の単位であり会社の所有を表す株式は，投資額に基づいて投資家に割り当てられます。株式を保有する株主は，株式数に応じて平等な扱いを受けます。例えば，株主総会における議決権は株式の数に応じて与えられます。

これに対して，株主は会社に対して義務および責任は負っていません。有限責任制度（Q4参照）により株主の責任は出資額とされていますが，株式を引き受けたときに出資の払込は完了しているので，株主となった後の責任は一切ありません。

Chapter Three : コーポレートガバナンス Corporate Governance

Q27 What rights, obligations and responsibilities do shareholders have?

A Shareholders have the right to share profitability and to take control over the company management. Shareholders do not have any obligations or responsibilities to the company.

The right to receive dividends is a typical right in sharing profitability. One of the most important rights to control the management is the right to cast votes in a shareholders' meeting. Since K.K. has a number of shareholders, directors operate the company on behalf of them. Shareholders control the management through the shareholders' meetings which make the most important decisions including selecting directors.

A share, a unit of investment expressing the ownership over the company, is allocated to investors based on the amount of their investment. Shareholders are treated equally based on the number of shares they have. For instance, voting rights at a shareholders' meeting are given to shareholders based on the number of shares they have.

In contrast, shareholders have no obligation or responsibility to the company. Under the limited liability protection (See Q4), the shareholder's responsibility is limited to the amount of their investments. Since the payment of the equity has been completed at the time of subscribing shares, there is no responsibility after becoming a shareholder.

85

Q28 株主総会にはどのような権限がありますか。

A 取締役会非設置会社の株主総会は，すべての事項を決定する権限がありますが，取締役会設置会社の株主総会が決議できる事項は，定款の変更や取締役の選任など重要な事項に限定されています。

　株主総会とは，株主によって構成され，会社の重要な事項を決定する機関です。「取締役会設置会社」の株主総会が決議できる事項は，定款変更，事業譲渡，取締役の選任・解任，取締役の報酬，計算書類の承認，配当の決定などがあります。株主に事前準備の機会を与えるために，株主総会の招集通知に記載されていなかった議題は株主総会で決議することはできません。株主総会において，質問を行う機会が与えられます。

　これに対して，「取締役会非設置会社」の株主総会はすべての事項を決定できます。招集通知に記載された議題以外でも，当日の株主総会で決議することができます。

Chapter Three：コーポレートガバナンス Corporate Governance

Q28　What powers does a shareholders' meeting have?

A　The shareholders' meeting of Company without Board of Directors has the authority to decide all matters. The matters that can be resolved by the shareholders' meeting of Company with Board of Directors are limited to important matters such as changes in the articles of incorporation and the director appointments.

A shareholders' meeting is a governing body which consists of all the shareholders, and decides important matters of the company's management.

Matters that can be resolved by the shareholders' meeting of a Company with Board of Directors include changes in the articles of incorporation, business transfer, director appointments and dismissals, director's compensation, approval of financial statements, and decision on dividends. The matters which are not notified by the invitation to the shareholders' meeting are not allowed to be resolved because shareholders should be given sufficient time for their contemplation. Shareholders are given opportunities to ask questions at a shareholders' meeting.

On the other hand, Company without Board of Directors allows its shareholders' meeting to decide all matters. Matters which are not informed by the invitation can be resolved at a shareholders' meeting.

Q29 株主総会はどうやって招集しますか。

A 株主が株主総会に出席する機会を確保するために，株主総会の招集方法は会社法により定められています。法定の招集方法を遵守しなければ，株主総会の決議が取り消されてしまう可能性があります。

「取締役会設置会社」の場合，取締役会が日時，場所，議題を決定し，これらを記載した招集通知を株主に発送します。計算書類を添付する必要があります。発送の期限は，公開会社は株主総会開催の2週間前，株式譲渡制限会社は1週間前となっています。招集通知は原則として書面で発送する必要がありますが，株主の承諾を得れば電子メールで発送することも可能です。株主全員の同意があれば招集手続自体を省略することができます。

「取締役会非設置会社」の場合，取締役が日時，場所，議題を決定し，これらを記載した招集通知を株主に発送します。発送の期限は株主総会開催の1週間前ですが，定款により1週間よりも短い期間に短縮することができます。招集通知は，書面や電子メールのほか，電話や口頭でも可能であり，計算書類を添付する必要はありません。また，招集通知に記載された議題以外でも，当日の株主総会で決議することができます。株主全員の同意があれば招集手続自体を省略することができます。

Chapter Three : コーポレートガバナンス Corporate Governance

Q29　How is a shareholders' meeting convened?

A　The way to convene a shareholders' meeting is prescribed by the Companies Act to secure the opportunities for shareholders to attend. If the company is in breach of statutory procedures, it would face a risk that resolutions made at the shareholders' meeting may be invalid.

In the case of Company with Board of Directors, the board decides and inform the date, venue, and agenda by the invitations to the shareholders. Financial statements are to be attached to the invitation, which must be sent out by two weeks before the shareholders' meeting. A Private Company is able to shorten the notice period to one week. An invitation is prepared in a paper form, but with an approval from a shareholder, it can be sent by email. The invitation process can be omitted if all the shareholders agree.

In the case of Company without Board of Directors, the directors decide and inform the date, venue, and agenda by the invitations to the shareholders. An invitation must be sent out by one week before the shareholders' meeting. It can be shortened if the articles of incorporation states so. An invitation can be prepared in the form of paper letter, email or even verbal communication. Financial statements are not necessarily to be attached. A shareholders' meeting can resolve any matters even if they are not informed by the invitation. The invitation process can be omitted if all the shareholders agree.

Q30　株主総会に外国親会社が実際に出席する必要はありますか。

A　電話会議による株主総会の開催が可能です。また，株主全員がその決議に賛成する場合には，株主総会を開催せずに書面（または電磁的記録）による決議を行うことができます。

　株主総会は親会社の本国で開催することも可能です。また，電話会議やテレビ会議システムにより複数の場所で開催することも可能です。例えば，株主は本国から，株主総会の議長を務める日本法人の代表取締役は日本から，電話会議による株主総会に参加することができます。

　また，株主全員がその決議に賛成する場合には，書面（または電磁的記録）による決議を行うことができます（会社法319条）。この方法で決議した場合，実際に株主総会を開催することはありませんが，株主総会議事録を作成しなければなりません（会社法施行規則72条4項1号）。

Chapter Three：コーポレートガバナンス Corporate Governance

Q34　How to determine the amounts of remuneration for directors?

A　The amount of remuneration is determined by an ordinary resolution at a shareholders' meeting.

If directors were able to decide the amount of their own remuneration, they might reward themselves large fees despite showing poor profits, which may cause damage to the company. Therefore, the amount of remuneration must be determined by the ordinary resolution at a shareholders' meeting. In the case of performance bonus linked to the profits of the company, the calculation method must be approved at the shareholders' meeting. The amount of remuneration can also be determined by the articles of incorporation, but it requires a special resolution at a shareholders' meeting to amend it.

It is commonly interpreted that it is valid to determine the upper limit of the total remuneration of directors instead of deciding each individual remuneration. In that case, the amount for each director will be determined by the board of directors. Instead of board's decision, it is allowed to make the representative director to decide the amount of each director. There is no need to update the resolution every year, unless the total amount of remuneration exceeds the limit.

Employees such as division managers and plant managers can concurrently serve as directors (employee-directors). If the company pays an employee's salary separate from director's fee, it is commonly interpreted that the employee's salary does not have to pass the resolution if 1) their payroll table is clearly established and 2) the company informs the shareholders that the director's fee does not include the employee's salary.

99

Q35 取締役が負う一般義務とはどのような義務ですか。

A 取締役は，一般義務として「善良な管理者の注意をもって職務にあたる義務」すなわち「善管注意義務」を負います。ただし，取締役が会社に成功をもたらす可能性が高いと善意に考えて行った行為については，結果として会社に損害を与えても，取締役の注意義務違反を問うべきではないという原則があります。

　会社法は，取締役に「忠実義務」を課しています（会社法355条）。そもそも，株式会社と委任関係にある取締役は，受任者の「善管注意義務」，すなわち「善良な管理者の注意をもって，委任事務を処理する義務」（民法644条）を負います。会社法が定める忠実義務は，民法が定める善管注意義務とは別個の義務を課したものではなく，善管注意義務を明確化したものと解されています。

　取締役は経営のプロとして期待される善管注意義務を負います。ただし，ビジネスの判断には失敗がつきものであり，その判断を事後的に評価して注意義務違反の責任を問うことは取締役の業務執行を委縮させることになります。そのため，取締役が会社に成功をもたらす可能性が高いと善意に考えて行った行為については，結果として会社に損害を与えたとしても，取締役の注意義務違反を問うべきではないという原則があります。したがって，注意義務違反が問われる局面とは，他の取締役・使用人に対する監督義務を怠った場合など任務懈怠が認められる場合です。

Chapter Three : コーポレートガバナンス Corporate Governance

Q35 What are the general duties of directors?

A As their general duties, directors are assigned to "a duty of care of a good manager". However, there is a legal principle that directors should not be blamed for losses that the company suffered as a result of their decisions and acts, if the decisions were based on good faith and were thought likely to promote success of the company.

The Companies Act sets out "a duty of loyalty (the Companies Act Article 355)" as the general duty directors must perform. Directors are deemed to enter into an agency agreement with the company when they take their offices. An agent is assigned "a duty of care of a good manager" set forth in Civil Code the article 644. Duty of loyalty is deemed as the same duty as a duty of care of a good manager.

Directors are required to perform their duties as professionals of management. However, business judgements made by directors are not always right in the business world. If directors were to be blamed for their lack of care at every bad outcome, they would hesitate to take their offices. Therefore, there is a legal principle that directors should not be blamed for losses that the company suffered as a result of their decisions and acts, if the decisions were based on good faith and were thought likely to promote success of the company. Directors are deemed being in breach of their duties if they neglect to oversee other directors and employees.

101

Q36 取締役が負う「競業避止義務」とはどのような義務ですか。

A 取締役が会社と同様の事業を自分自身で行おうとするときは，その取引に関する重要事項を示したうえで，取締役会の承認を得る義務があります。

　取締役が会社と同様の事業を行うと，会社のノウハウや顧客を不正に利用し，会社に不当な損害を与えるおそれがあります。そこで，取締役が自己または第三者のために会社と同様の事業を行おうとするときは，その取引に関する重要事項を示したうえで，取締役会（取締役会非設置会社は株主総会）の承認を得る必要があります（会社法356条1項1号，365条1項）。

　取締役が，同様の事業を行う他社の代表取締役に就任することも競業にあたります。会社の取締役が同様の事業を行う子会社の代表取締役に就任することがありますが，完全親子関係にある場合には，子会社の利益はすべて親会社の利益となるため，承認は不要と解されています。一方，同様の事業を行う合弁会社に取締役を派遣し，同社の代表取締役に就任させるには，承認が必要です。

　承認を得ずに会社と同様の事業を行った場合，取締役が得た利益が会社に生じた損失額であると推定されます（会社法423条2項）。これによって，取締役に対する損害賠償請求の訴訟において，会社が損失の額を立証する必要がなくなります。なお，会社の承認を得た場合でも，会社に損害が発生したときには，会社から損害賠償請求を受ける可能性があることには留意が必要です。

Chapter Three : コーポレートガバナンス Corporate Governance

Q36　What is directors' "Non-compete obligation" ?

A　If directors want to start a similar business to that of the company, they need to disclose the essence of their business plan and obtain permission from the company's board of directors.

If a director starts a similar business, the company would face the risk of the director gaining competitive advantage by exploiting confidential information including know-how and client lists, which would cause damage to the company. To avoid such misconduct, directors are required by law to disclose the essence of their business plan and obtain permission from the board of directors of the company (the shareholders' meeting in the case of Company without Board of Directors), when directors start a similar business not only for their own but also another person's interests (the Companies Act Article 356(1)(i), 365(1)).

Holding office of a representative director of another company which conducts a similar business falls under the competitive behavior. Directors of companies are often appointed as representative directors of their subsidiaries, which conduct similar businesses. If the parent company holds 100% of the shares in the subsidiary, an approval is not necessary since all the interests of subsidiary belongs to its parent company. On the other hand, if directors of companies are appointed as representative directors of joint venture companies, approvals are required.

If directors start similar businesses without approvals, it is deemed that the profits gained by them equal the amount of losses caused to the companies (the Companies Act Article 423(2)). This relieves the companies from proving the amount of losses in law suits. It should be noted that even if the company's approval is obtained, the company may claim the loss if they suffer damages.

103

Q37 取締役による「利益相反取引」とは何ですか。

A 取締役が会社と行う取引は，会社の利益を犠牲にして自分の利益を図ろうとするおそれが常にあることから，利益相反取引と呼ばれます。利益相反取引を行おうとする取締役は，会社に対してその取引に関する重要事項を示したうえで，取締役会（取締役会非設置会社の場合は株主総会）の承認を得る義務があります。

取締役が会社と取引を行うと，会社の利益を犠牲にして自分の利益を図ろうとするおそれがあります。そこで，取締役が自己または第三者のために会社と取引を行おうとするときは，その取引に関する重要事項を示したうえで，取締役会（取締役会非設置会社の場合は株主総会）の承認を得る必要があります（会社法356条1項2号）。ただし，会社が取締役から無利息・無担保で貸付を受けるなど，会社に損害が生じえない取引については，承認は不要です。

会社の取締役が子会社の代表取締役を兼務している場合，子会社との取引は利益相反取引にあたります。反復継続して取引を行うのであれば，包括的に承認を得ておくことが可能です。

会社が取締役の債務を保証するなど，取締役以外の者との取引であっても，会社と取締役の間で利益が相反する取引は規制の対象になります（会社法356条1項3号）。

承認を得なかった場合の取引の有効性について，会社法は規定を設けていませんが，会社は取引の無効を主張することができると解されています。ただし，判例によれば，取引の相手方が取締役以外の第三者の場合，取引の安全の観点から，会社が，①相手方が取引は利益相反取引にあたることを知っていたこと，

Chapter Three：コーポレートガバナンス Corporate Governance

Q37 What is directors' "Conflict-of-interest transactions"?

A Transactions that a director of a company makes with the company are called conflict-of-interest transactions, because there is always a possibility that the director will try to make their own profits at the expense of the company.

A director who wishes to make a deal with the company are obliged to obtain the approval of the board of directors (in the case of a Company without Board of Directors, shareholders' meeting) after presenting the company with important matters concerning the transaction (the Companies Act Article 356(1)(ii)). An approval is not required for transactions that do not harm the company such as a loan to the company with no interests and collaterals.

If a director of a company concurrently serves as a representative director of the subsidiary of the company, deals that the company makes with the subsidiary are conflicts-of-interest transactions as well. If the company plans on repeating the transactions, you may want to obtain comprehensive approval.

A deal with the third party can be a conflict-of-interest transaction. For instance, if a company guarantees the debt of the director, such deal is subject to the conflict-of-interest regulations (the Companies Act Article 356(1)(iii)).

The Companies Act does not say anything about the validity of the transaction that are done without the approval, but it is common opinion that the company can claim the invalidation of the transaction. However, according to the judicial precedent, in the case that the counterparty of the

105

②相手方が取締役会等の承認を得ていないことを知っていたことを立証した場合に限り，会社は無効を主張できるとされています。

　なお，利益相反取引によって会社に損害が生じた際には，①取引を行った取締役，②利益相反取引の承認に賛成した取締役は，任務を怠ったと推定されます（会社法423条3項）。あくまで推定が働くだけなので，取締役側で反証できれば責任を免れることができます（立証責任を会社ではなく取締役に負わせていることに意義があります）。ただし，取引を行った取締役は，たとえ「任務を怠ったことが当該取締役の責めに帰することができない事由によるもの」であったときでも損害賠償責任を負います（無過失責任）。

Chapter Three : コーポレートガバナンス Corporate Governance

transaction is a third party, the company can claim the invalidation only if the company can prove that the counterparty knew 1) that the transaction falls under conflict-of-transaction, and 2) that the approval was not obtained.

If the company suffers damage as a result of the conflict-of-interest transactions, directors 1) who made the transactions, and 2) who voted for approval on the transaction, are presumed to have neglected their duties (the Companies Act Article 423(3)). As this is just presumption, directors will not be liable if they can prove otherwise (the legal burden of proof is on the director). However, directors who made the conflict-of-interest transactions are always liable even if they prove that the failure to perform their duty is not attributed to their fault (strict liability).

107

Q38 取締役は会社に対してどのような責任を負いますか。

A 取締役は，一般義務として会社に対して善管注意義務を負っています（Q35参照）。任務を怠ったことで会社に損害を発生させた場合は，会社に対して損害賠償責任を負います（会社法423条1項）。さらに，一定の重要な事項については，次のように加重された責任を負っています。

(1) 利益相反取引

利益相反取引を行った取締役は，たとえ「任務を怠ったことが当該取締役の責めに帰することができない事由によるもの」であったと立証できたとしても無過失責任を負います（Q37参照）。

(2) 株主に対する利益供与

「株式会社は，何人に対しても，株主の権利の行使に関し，利益の供与をしてはならない」とされています。これはいわゆる総会屋対策のために設けられた規定です。例えば，反社会勢力から金銭の要求があり，要求に応じないと会社の株式を取得したうえで株主権を行使して会社の不正を暴くといった脅しがあった場合，利益供与に関与した取締役は連帯して供与した利益の価額に相当する額を会社に対して支払う義務を負います。ただし，その取締役（利益の供与をした取締役を除く）がその職務を行うについて注意を怠らなかったことを証明した場合は免除されます（会社法120条4項）。

(3) 違法配当

分配可能額を超えて剰余金を配当した場合，取締役は配当を受けた株主と連帯して会社に返還する義務があります。ただし，職務を行うことについて注意

Chapter Three : コーポレートガバナンス Corporate Governance

Q38　What makes directors liable to the company?

A　As general duties to be performed, directors are assigned to a duty of care (See Q35). If directors cause damage to the company due to neglect of their duties, they will be held liable to the company for it. In addition, directors may incur weighed liabilities for certain critical matters as follows.

(1) Conflict-of-interest transaction

Strict liability will be imposed on directors who made the conflict-of-interest transactions, even if they prove that the failure to perform their duties is not attributed to their fault (See Q37).

(2) Benefits given to shareholders

The Companies Act stipulates that "a company shall not give any benefits to any person regarding the exercise of shareholders' rights." This clause has been introduced in order to shut out corporate racketeers. For example, in the case where anti-social forces demand for money by threatening to exercise shareholder rights to disclose the company's fraud, directors involved in giving benefits shall be jointly liable to the company for the amount equivalent to the value of the benefit given, unless directors (excluding the directors who actually gave such benefit) prove they did not fail to exercise due care with respect to the performance of their duties (the Companies Act Article 120(4)).

(3) Illegal distribution of dividends

If a company distributes dividends excessing the distributable amount, directors and shareholders who received the dividends are jointly liable to return the dividends back to the company. If the directors prove that due

109

を怠らなかったことを取締役が証明したときは弁済義務を負いません。

(4) 現物出資・仮装払込

　金銭ではなく不動産など現物財産で出資することが認められていますが，実際の価値より高い価額で評価して出資すると，資本金に相当する資産が会社に払い込まれていないことになり，資本金の金額を信用して取引を行った債権者を害することになります。そのため，現物出資に関わった取締役に対して，検査役の調査を受けていた場合を除き，取締役が無過失を証明しない限り，出資者と連帯して不足額を会社に対して支払う責任を負わせています。

　また，出資を受けた直後に株主に対して出資金を貸し出す行為も，債権者に対して害がおよびます。このような行為を「仮装払込」といいます。仮装払込に関与した取締役は，無過失を証明しない限り，当該出資をした株主と連帯して会社に対して仮装した出資額を支払う責任を負わせています。

Chapter Three：コーポレートガバナンス Corporate Governance

care with respect to their duties was exercised, they are not liable for such damage.

(4) Contribution in kind and Disguise payment

Instead of cash injection, shareholders can invest with assets such as real estate. However, if the assets are overvalued, it means that the asset equivalent to the capital amount has not been paid to the company, which would harm creditors accordingly, who believed the capital amount is true when they made a deal with the company. Except for the case that statutory inspector was engaged in the evaluation process, directors are liable to pay the shortage amount to the company jointly with the shareholders who made the contribution, unless the director proves no negligence.

Another harmful transaction is lending money to shareholders after the capital injection. This transaction is called "disguise payment". Directors involved in the disguise payment are liable to pay the disguised amount to the company jointly with the shareholders who borrowed, unless the directors prove that they did not fail to exercise due care with respect to their duties.

Q39　株主は違法行為をした取締役を訴えることができますか？

A　株主は，会社に違法行為をした取締役の責任を追及する訴えを起こすよう請求し，会社が請求から60日以内に訴えを起こさない場合には，株主自らが会社を代表して訴えを起こすことができます（株主代表訴訟）。また，完全子会社の取締役に対して株主代表訴訟を起こすことも可能です。

　取締役が任務を懈怠することによって会社に損害を与えた場合，会社は取締役に対して損害賠償を請求することになります。しかし，他の取締役が仲間意識から当該取締役の責任を追及しない可能性があります。そこで，株主が会社を代表して取締役に対して提訴することが認められています。これを，株主代表訴訟といいます。6カ月前から引き続き株式を有する株主であれば，1株でも株主代表訴訟を起こすことができます。会社に取締役に対する訴えを起こすよう請求し，それに対して会社が訴えを起こさない場合には，株主が会社を代表して訴えを起こすことができます。

　また，株主は会社の完全子会社の取締役に対しても，株主代表訴訟を起こすことが認められています。子会社の取締役が任務懈怠によって子会社に損害を与えた場合，親会社は子会社の株主として取締役に株主代表訴訟を提起することが可能ですが，仲間意識からそのような訴えを提起しないおそれがあります。そこで，親会社の株主が親会社の取締役に対して親会社の監督責任を追及する株主代表訴訟を起こすことが考えられますが，監督責任を立証することは難しいことから，親会社の株主が100%子会社の取締役を直接訴えることが認められています（多重代表訴訟）。

Chapter Three : コーポレートガバナンス Corporate Governance

Q39 Are shareholders able to sue directors for wrongful acts?

A Shareholders have the right to demand the company to sue directors for wrongful act. If the company does not take any action within 60 days from the request, the shareholders are authorized to sue directors on behalf of the company (shareholder derivative lawsuit). Shareholders are also allowed to sue directors of a subsidiary 100% owned by the company.

If a director neglects his duties and gives damages to the company accordingly, the company is supposed to demand them to indemnify for its losses. However, other directors may be unwilling to sue their colleagues. So, shareholders are able to bring lawsuits against directors on behalf of the company. This is called "shareholder derivative suit". A shareholder who continues to hold a share for at least six months have the right to initiate a lawsuit. A shareholder may first petition the company to proceed with legal action. If the company does not take any action, the shareholder may take it upon himself to bring an action on behalf of the company.

Shareholders are also allowed to file lawsuits against directors of wholly-owned subsidiary of the company. In the first place, the parent company should take legal actions as the shareholder of the subsidiary, if a director of the subsidiary causes harm to the subsidiary due to his neglect. However, such lawsuit may not be brought due to a sense of fellowship. Even if shareholders of the parent company decide to file a derivative suit to accuse directors of the parent company for not supervising the subsidiary, it is difficult for shareholders to prove that the directors have neglected supervisory duties. Therefore, the Companies Act allows shareholders to directly sue the directors of wholly owned subsidiaries (multiple derivative lawsuit).

113

Q40 取締役は会社が第三者に与えた損害に対して直接責任を負いますか。

A 会社が第三者に与えた損害について，取締役がその職務を行うにあたって故意または重過失があったときは，その取締役は第三者に対して損害賠償の責任を負います。

取締役が会社の行為として取引先など第三者に損害を与えたときには，会社が第三者に対して責任を負います。損害を賠償した会社は，取締役に任務懈怠が認められる場合には，取締役に対して損害賠償を請求します。

これに対して，取締役に故意または重大な過失があったときは，取締役は第三者に対して直接責任を負うこととされています。これは，株式会社の経済社会に占める地位および取締役の職務の重要性を考慮し，第三者保護の立場から取締役に厳しい責任を負わせたものとされています。

さらに，事実ではない情報を開示したことによって第三者に損害が生じた場合には，取締役に立証責任を転嫁しています。すなわち取締役が無過失であることを自ら立証しないかぎり，第三者に対して損害賠償責任を負います。不実の情報開示には以下のものがあります。

- 株式の募集を行う際に虚偽の通知を行った場合
- 虚偽の決算書を作成した場合
- 虚偽の登記を行った場合

Chapter Three : コーポレートガバナンス Corporate Governance

Q40 Are directors liable to third parties for damages caused by the company?

A Directors will be immediately and personally liable to third parties for damages caused by the company if the directors committed actionable wrongs intentionally or by gross negligence.

A company is liable to the third party when directors of the company have damaged the third party as a result of their duty. And then, the company may claim the directors for the compensation if neglection of their duties have caused the damages.

If a director committed or directed actionable wrongs intentionally or by gross negligence, they will be immediately liable to the third party. From the standpoint of third-party protection, directors are required to undertake strict responsibilities, considering the status of companies in the economic society and the importance of director's duties.

Furthermore, in the case that a third party is damaged by the company disclosing false information, the legal burden of proof is on the directors. The directors will be liable to the third party unless they prove that they are not at fault. False information disclosure includes:

- False information about public offering of shares
- False financial statements
- False Company registrations

115

▶取締役会

Q41 取締役会にはどのような権限が与えられていますか。

A 取締役会は，①会社の業務執行を決定する，②代表取締役を含むすべての取締役の職務の執行を監督する，③代表取締役の選定および解職を行う，の３つの権限を有します（会社法362条）。

取締役会は，法令・定款により株主総会の決議事項とされた事項を除き，会社の業務執行すべてについて決定する権限を有しています。日常の個々の業務執行の決定は業務執行取締役に委任することができますが，「重要な財産の処分・譲受け」「多額の借財」「支配人など重要な使用人の選任・解任」など，法令で定められた事項は，業務執行取締役に決定を委ねることができず，必ず取締役会の決議が必要になります。

取締役会が決定した業務は，取締役会が選任した代表取締役が執行します。取締役会は代表取締役を含むすべての取締役の職務の執行を監督し，不適任と認めた場合には代表取締役を解職することができます（代表取締役は代表権を失うにすぎず，取締役としての地位は継続します。取締役の解任は株主総会の権限です）。モニタリングのために，代表取締役は３カ月に１度以上，職務の執行状況を取締役会に報告しなければなりません。

116

Chapter Three：コーポレートガバナンス Corporate Governance

Q41　What powers does a board of directors have?

A　A board of directors has three powers: 1) making decisions on the company's business operations, 2) supervising the performance of all directors, 3) electing and dismissing representative directors (the Companies Act Article 362).

A board of directors resolves all the matters regarding the company's business operations, except for the statutory matters which require a resolution of the shareholders' meeting in accordance with the provisions of the Companies Act or the articles of incorporation. A board of directors is allowed to delegate decision-making powers on day-to-day operations to executive directors. However, decisions on statutory matters including "Disposal and transfer of important properties" "Significant amount of debt" "Appointment and dismissal of important employees" must be resolved by a resolution of the board of directors.

Decisions made by a board of directors are executed by the representative directors elected by the board. The board of directors oversees the performance of all directors including representative directors, and dismisses them if they are unfit for their post (Representative directors only lose the role and power of representation, and they remain as directors. Dismissal of directors are done by a resolution of shareholders' meeting.)　As a part of the monitoring system, representative directors must report to the board of directors on the status of business at least every three months.

117

Q42 取締役会はどうやって招集しますか。

A 開催の1週間前までに招集通知を発送する必要がありますが，定款で期間を短縮できます。なお，取締役会に参加するものが全員同意した場合は，招集手続を省略することができます。

　各取締役は取締役会を招集できます。ただし，取締役会を招集する取締役を定款または取締役会で定めた場合は，当該取締役がこれを招集します。招集権を有しない取締役は，招集権を有する取締役に対して，取締役会の目的である事項を示して取締役会を招集するよう請求することができます。請求があった日から5日以内に取締役会の招集通知が発せられない場合，この請求をした取締役は自ら取締役会を招集することができます。

　監査役および株主も取締役会の開催を取締役に対して請求することができますが，株主が請求できるのは，取締役が定款に違反する行為を行った場合など一定の理由がある場合に限られます。

Chapter Three：コーポレートガバナンス Corporate Governance

Q42　How to convene a board meeting?

A　A board meeting will be convened by the convocation notice to all attendees no later than one week before the meeting, which can be shortened by the articles of incorporation. The convocation notice can be omitted by unanimous consent of all attendees.

Each director is able to convene a board meeting. The articles of incorporation or the board of directors can designate the convening officers from directors. Directors without the convocation right will inform the agenda to the designated directors to request to convene a meeting. If convocation notice is not issued within five days from the date of the request, the director who made the request is able to convene a meeting.

Corporate Auditors and shareholders can also request directors to hold a board of directors meeting. Shareholders can demand only if they have certain reasons such as when directors violate the articles of incorporation.

119

Q43　取締役会はどうやって決議を行いますか。

A　取締役会の決議は，議決に加わることができる取締役の過半数が出席し（定足数），その過半数をもって行います（決議要件）。定款によって，定足数と決議要件を加重することができますが，軽減することはできません。

　電話会議やテレビ会議で取締役会を行うことは問題ありません。定款に定めれば，取締役全員が書面（または電磁的記録）で議案に賛成する意思表示をした場合には，監査役が当該提案について異議を述べたときを除き，会議の開催がなくても取締役会の決議があったものとみなすことができます。また，取締役会への報告事項についても，取締役全員に通知した場合は，取締役会での報告は省略できます。ただし，代表取締役および業務執行取締役の職務執行に関する報告（Q41参照）は，通知ではなく取締役会で報告しなければなりません。したがって，少なくとも３カ月に１度は取締役会を開催しなければなりません。

Chapter Three : コーポレートガバナンス Corporate Governance

Q43　How does a board of directors make a decision?

A　A board of directors makes a decision by a majority of the votes of the directors present at a board meeting (the voting requirement). A board meeting is constituted with the attendance of a majority of directors who are eligible to cast their votes (the quorum). The voting requirement and the quorum can be weighed by the articles of incorporation, but not relaxed.

Board meetings can be held through telephone or video conference. The article of incorporation allows boards of directors to make a decision without holding a meeting. Decisions are deemed to be made when all directors unanimously consent in writing (or by electromagnetic record) without holding a meeting if corporate auditors do not express any objections. Also, statutory report to the board of directors can be made by sending to each director instead of reporting at a board meeting. However, the report of the business from representative directors must be made at a board meeting (See Q41) Therefore, it must be held at least every three month.

121

▶*代表取締役*

Q44 代表取締役にはどのような権限が与えられていますか。

A 代表取締役は，会社の業務を執行し，対外的には，会社を代表して第三者と取引を締結する代表権を有します。

　意思決定機関と執行機関を分離している取締役会設置会社は，業務執行機関として代表取締役を必ず設置しなければなりません。取締役会によって取締役のなかから選任された代表取締役は，取締役会が決定した事項を執行するとともに，日常業務については，取締役会によって任された範囲において，代表取締役が自ら意思決定を行います。対外的には，代表権（Q45参照）が与えられ，会社を代表して第三者と契約を締結することができます。

　「取締役会非設置会社」においては，すべての取締役が代表取締役となります。特定の取締役だけに代表権を与えることも可能です。

Chapter Three : コーポレートガバナンス Corporate Governance

Q44 What powers do representative directors have?

A Representative directors execute the business of the company, and have the authority to represent the company when dealing with third parties.

A Company with Board of Directors, which separates the powers into decision-making branch and executive branch, is required to elect representative directors as executive branch. Representative directors, elected among directors by the board of directors, execute what the board decided, and make decisions on day-to-day operations to the extent that the board delegates. Representative directors are given the authority to represent the company (See Q45), and make a deal with third parties as a representative of the company.

Every director of a Company without Board of Directors is a representative director. You can give the authority to represent the company only to certain directors.

123

Q45 代表権とはどのような権限ですか。

A 代表権とは，会社を代表する権限で，代表権を持つもの（代表者）が行った取引行為は会社に帰属します。

　会社が第三者と契約するといっても，実際に契約書に押印またはサインするのは，社長や部長，従業員などの個人です。したがって，その個人が契約を締結する権限を持っているか確認する必要があります。

　一般的な代理権では，その取引を代理する権限が会社から与えられているかどうか確かめなければなりません。これに対して，代表権を持つ代表者の氏名と住所は登記事項とされており，代表者の印鑑は法務局に登録されています。登記簿と印鑑証明書によって，相手方が会社の代表者であるかどうか容易に確認でき，契約書に押印された代表者の印鑑の真正性を確かめることができます。

　代表権は取締役に与えられるものですが，会社が契約を締結する権限を従業員に包括的に与える方法として，支配人制度と特定委任制度があります。

　支配人とは，会社の本店または支店の事業を行うために選任される使用人で，担当する本店または支店の業務に関する一切の行為を代理する権限が与えられます（会社法10条）。支配人は登記簿で確かめることができます。

　特定委任とは，事業に関するある種類または特定の事項に関して，一切の裁判外の行為を包括的に代理する権限を与える制度です（会社法14条）。特定委任を受けた者かどうかは登記簿では確認できないので，必要に応じて，委任状の提示を求めるべきといえます。

124

Chapter Three：コーポレートガバナンス Corporate Governance

Q45 What is the "authority to represent the company"?

A The authority to represent the company is the power of representing a company, and any transactional acts performed by the persons with this authority (a representative) belong to the company.

When a company enters into a contract with a third party, deals are actually sealed by signatures or seals of natural persons such as presidents, managers, and employees.

You should confirm that your counterpart has the authority given by the company every time you make a deal. If your counterpart is a representative of the company, you will find his name and residential address on the company register. Moreover, his seal is registered with the Legal Affairs Bureau. With a copy of the company register and the certificate of the registered seal, you can confirm that your counterparty has the authority to represent the company, and verify the authenticity of the seal stamped on the contract.

Authority to represent the company can only be given to directors. However, there are two ways to give employees a comprehensive authority to make a deal.

General manager (the Companies Act Article 10) is an employee who is given a comprehensive authority to make a deal with third parties on behalf of the head office or branch office he is in charge of. The name of general managers is registered on the company register.

Companies can also give a comprehensive authority on specific areas of the business except for legal actions (the Companies Act Article 14). Persons with this type of authority is not shown on the company register, so you should confirm by a power of attorney.

125

Q46 取締役会の決議を経ないで代表取締役が行った取引は無効になりますか。

A 取締役会の決議を経ないで代表取締役が行った取引の効力について明確に規定する条文はありません。取引が無効となるかどうかはケースごとに判断するしかありません。

法令で取締役会の決議が必要な事項，例えば「重要な財産の処分・譲受け」について取締役会の決議を経ないで代表取締役が独断で取引を行った場合，会社はその取引を取り消すことができるでしょうか。

取締役会決議を欠いた重要財産の処分について，原則として有効であるが，取引の相手方が取締役会の決議が必要であることを知っていた，または，知りえた場合には無効とする判決があります。

一方，株主総会の決議が必要な「事業譲渡」について，株主総会の決議を経ないで取引を行った場合，無効とした判例があります。それに対して，有効な決議を欠いた「株式の発行」について，株式を引き受けた株主の取引の安全を重視して有効とした判例があります。

Chapter Three : コーポレートガバナンス Corporate Governance

Q46 If a representative director makes a deal without a necessary resolution of the board of directors, is the deal deemed as void?

A The Companies Act has no provisions about the effectiveness of such misconduct. It depends on the case whether the deal is deemed to be void or not.

A resolution of the board of directors is required by law for some important transactions such as dispose/acquire of important assets. The question is whether or not a company can void the transactions, if they were made by its representative director without a resolution of the board.

There is a legal precedent where disposal of important assets without resolution of the board was regarded valid unless the counterparty knew or should have known that the transaction would require a resolution of the board of directors.

On the other hand, there is a case where "business transfer (selling a division of the company)", which requires shareholders' resolution, was judged invalid because of the lack of valid resolution. To the contrary, another precedent shows that issuance of shares without a valid resolution was not void, weighing the safety of the transactions for new shareholders who already purchased shares.

127

▶監査役

Q47 監査役とはどのような役職ですか。

A 監査役は，取締役の職務執行を監査する会社の役員です。

　取締役会設置会社のコーポレートガバナンスのポイントは，業務の意思決定機関である取締役会が，業務執行を行う取締役を監視することにあります。ところが，日本の経営実態として，取締役会のほとんどを社内の業務執行取締役が占めており，取締役会は業務執行取締役を監督する機能を十分にはたしていないという批判があります。そのため，取締役会の監督機能を補うために監査役制度が導入されています。日本独特のダブルモニタリングシステムである監査役は，英語ではCorporate AuditorまたはAudit & Supervisory Board Memberと訳されています。監査役は取締役の職務執行を監査する株主に任命された会社の役員です。取締役会設置会社は監査役の設置が義務づけられており，取締役会非設置会社は任意で導入することが可能です。

　監査役の設置に代えて，他の「監査等委員会設置会社」または「指名委員会等設置会社」という他の2つのモニタリングシステムを選ぶこともできます。

Chapter Three : コーポレートガバナンス Corporate Governance

$Q47$ What is a Corporate Auditor?

A A Corporate Auditor is a company officer who has the duty to audit the directors' performance of duties.

Essence of corporate governance at Company with Board of Directors is that the executive directors are closely monitored by the board of directors. However, there has been a criticism that companies appoint few external non-executive directors, and executive directors occupy most seats of the board, which is interfering the monitoring function of the board. To backup monitoring system, Kansayaku was introduced. Kansayaku is a double monitoring system unique to Japan, which is translated to "Corporate Auditor" or "Audit & Supervisory Board Member". Appointed by shareholders, as an officer of the company Corporate Auditors have a role to audit directors. Company with Board of Directors must appoint Corporate Auditors while it is optional for Company without Board of Directors to appoint them.

Instead of appointing corporate auditors, the company can choose from two other options as its monitoring system, "Company with Audit Committee" and "Company with Nominating Committee".

129

Q48　監査役はどのような職務を行いますか。

A　監査役の職務は，取締役の職務を監査することです。株主に監査結果を報告するため，監査報告書を株主総会に報告する義務があります。

　監査には業務監査と会計監査の２つの監査があります。業務監査では，取締役の業務執行が法令に違反していないかを監査します。取締役の活動を監視するために監査役は取締役会に出席する義務があります。株式譲渡制限会社では，少数の株主が取締役を直接監視することが可能なこともあるので，監査役の権限を会計監査だけに限定することが認められています。

　会計監査では，取締役が作成した会社の財務諸表が適切に作成されているかを確かめます。資本金が５億円以上または負債が200億円以上の会社（大会社）は，監査のうち会計監査について，会計専門家の資格を有する公認会計士または監査法人を会社の機関の１つである会計監査人として選任する必要があります。その場合，監査役は自ら会計監査は行わず，会計監査人の監査結果が相当であることについて監査意見を述べます。

Chapter Three : コーポレートガバナンス Corporate Governance

Q48 What duties do Corporate Auditors have?

A The duties of the Corporate Auditors are to audit the duties performed by directors of the company. In order to report the audit results to shareholders, Corporate Auditors submit the audit report to the shareholders' meeting.

Corporate Auditors conduct two types of audit, operational audit and financial audit. To perform operational audit, Corporate Auditors monitor the performance of directors' duties and ensure that they are not involved in any misconduct. Corporate Auditors are required to attend board meetings for monitoring purpose. Private Company, a company with a small number of shareholders, is allowed to limit the scope of audit to financial audit only, as shareholders may be able to monitor the directors directly by themselves.

Corporate Auditors also conduct financial audit on the company's financial statements prepared by the directors. Large companies with capital of JPY 500 million or more or with liabilities of JPY 20 billion or more are required to appoint a certified public accountant or an audit corporation as an Accounting Auditor, which is a company's officer. Corporate Auditors would not conduct financial audit work by themselves. They only review the results of financial audit conducted by the Accounting Auditor and express their opinion whether the external audit was performed appropriately or not.

131

Q49 監査役の選任・解任はどのように行いますか。

A 監査役は株主総会の普通決議で選任されますが，解任するには特別決議が必要です。

　監査役は株主総会の普通決議で選任されます。監査役の人数は定款で自由に決めることができます。監査役は取締役や使用人を兼ねることができません。非居住者でも監査役に就任できるため，本国の親会社の役職員を日本法人の監査役に任命して日本法人の取締役会を監視するケースが多いと思われます。監査役の任期は4年ですが，株式譲渡制限会社は10年まで伸長することができます。監査役も取締役と同じく株主総会で解任できますが，取締役と異なり，普通決議ではなく特別決議が必要です。

Chapter Three : コーポレートガバナンス Corporate Governance

Q49 How are Corporate Auditors elected and dismissed?

A Corporate Auditors will be appointed by an ordinary resolution of the general meeting of shareholders. A special resolution is necessary to dismiss Corporate Auditors.

Corporate Auditors will be elected by an ordinary resolution of the general meeting of shareholders. The number of Corporate Auditors is determined by the articles of incorporation. Corporate Auditors cannot concurrently serve as directors or employees. As non-residents can be appointed as Corporate Auditors, officers or employees of the parent company in the home country are often appointed as Corporate Auditors to monitor the board of directors of the Japan subsidiary. The term of office of Corporate Auditors is four years. Private companies can extend it up to ten years. Corporate Auditors are dismissed at the shareholders' meeting by passing a special resolution.

133

▶▶合同会社のコーポレートガバナンス

Q50　合同会社のコーポレートガバナンスの特徴は何でしょうか。

A　合同会社は，少数の出資者が自ら会社を経営することを想定した会社です。出資者と会社の関係を規律するコーポレートガバナンスの多くは，定款に記載する方法で自由に設計することが可能です。

　合同会社の出資者は「社員」と呼ばれ，会社の業務を執行する権利と義務を有します。ただし，定款で定めれば，一部の社員だけに業務を執行させることができます。業務を執行する社員は「業務執行社員」といい，対外的に代表権（Q44参照）を持ちますが，一部の社員だけに代表権を持たせることもできます。代表権を持つ社員を「代表社員」といいます。法人が社員の場合は，実際に職務執行を行う自然人を任命します。

　重要な意思決定を行う場合は業務執行社員の過半数の合意が必要ですが，定款で意思決定の方法を変更することが可能です。意思決定方法の定め方については特に制限がないため，例えば，業務執行社員の過半数ではなく全員の同意を必要としたり，特定の1人の社員に決定権を委ねたりすることも可能です。意思決定の際に，株式会社の株主総会や取締役会のような正式な会議を開く必要はありません。

　このように，社員と会社の関係を規律するコーポレートガバナンスの多くは，定款に記載する方法で自由に設計することが可能です。定款の変更は原則として社員全員の同意が必要ですが，過半数で変更できると定款で定めることも可能です。

Chapter Three : コーポレートガバナンス Corporate Governance

Q50　How is G.K. governed?

A　G.K. is designed for a few investors to operate the company on their own. Most of the corporate governance disciplines which govern the relationship between investors and the company can be modified flexibly by describing in the articles of incorporation.

Investors in G.K. are called "members", who are all given the rights and duties to run the business of the company. It is possible to limit the role of operating business to certain members by describing in the articles of incorporation. Members who operate the business are called "executive members." Executive members have the authority to represent the company (See Q44). It is also possible to give the representative authority only to certain executive members. Executive members who represent the company are called "Representative members." If a member is a corporate, a natural person who actually performs the job will be appointed.

It requires a majority of the votes of executive members when you make important decisions. However, the way of decision making can be changed by describing in the articles of incorporation. The law has no particular restriction on internal rules to be set, it is allowed, for example, to require the consent of all executive members instead of a majority of votes, or to delegate the decision-making power to a certain member. Official meetings such as a shareholders' meeting and a board meeting at K.K. are not necessary to be held when you make decisions.

In this way, most of the corporate governance disciplines which govern the relationship between members and the company can be modified flexibly by describing in the articles of incorporation. You can even change the way to revise the articles of incorporation. For example, the default setting for revising the articles of incorporation requires the consent of all members, but you can change it to a majority of votes by describing in the articles of incorporation.

135

Q51 業務執行社員はどのような義務を負いますか。

A 合同会社の業務執行社員は，会社に対して株式会社の取締役と同様の善管注意義務を負います。

業務執行社員は，会社に対して善管注意義務（Q35参照）を負います。業務執行社員が善管注意義務を欠くことによって会社に損害が発生した場合，業務執行社員は会社に対して賠償する義務を負いますが，会社は免除することが可能です。株式会社と比べより自由に免除の方法を定款で定めることが可能です。

競業取引（Q36参照）の承認を得るには，他の社員全員の同意が必要です。ただし，定款によって異なる承認方法を定めることが可能です。株式会社と同様に，承認を得ずに会社と同様の事業を行った場合，業務執行社員が得た利益が会社に生じた損失額であると推定されます。

利益相反取引（Q37参照）の承認は，他の社員の過半数の同意で足り，定款によって承認方法を定めることが可能です。

株式会社の取締役と同様に，会社が第三者に与えた損害について，業務執行社員がその職務を行うにあたって故意または重過失があったときは，その業務執行社員は第三者に対して損害賠償の責任を負います（Q40参照）。

136

Chapter Three : コーポレートガバナンス Corporate Governance

Q51 What duties do executive members have?

A Executive members of G.K. have the same duty to the company as directors of K.K., which is the duty of care of a good manager.

Executive members have the duty of care of a good manager (See Q35). If an executive member neglects the duty and causes damage to the company, the member is liable to compensate for those damages. The company can exempt the member from the liability. G.K. is allowed to set its own rules on how to exempt in the article of incorporation, more freely than K.K.

Permission which is required by non-compete obligation (See Q36) will be given with the consent of all the other executive members. It is possible to change the way of giving permissions by describing in the articles of incorporation. If executive members conduct similar businesses without approval from the company, they lead to the same outcome as K.K. It is estimated that the profit gained by the executive member is equivalent to the amount of losses caused to the company.

An approval for conflict-of-interest transaction (See Q37) requires agreement from the majority of other members. The way of approval can be changed if you state it in the articles of incorporation.

In the same manner as K.K., executive members of G.K. will be liable directly to third parties for damages caused by the company, if the executive members committed actionable wrongs intentionally or by gross negligence (See Q40).

137

▶▶支店のコーポレートガバナンス

Q52　支店のコーポレートガバナンスの特徴は何でしょうか。

A　会社法は，本店と支店の関係を規律する規定は特段設けていません。支店のコーポレートガバナンスは企業の内部のルールによって運営されるべきものと言えます。

　支店は本店から法的に独立した企業体ではないため，支店と本店の利害対立について法令で解決する必要性はありません。支店が得た利益と本店が被った損失は同じリーガルエンティティに帰属するからです。したがって，会社法は，本店と支店の関係を規律する規定は特段設けておらず，支店のコーポレートガバナンスは企業の内部のルールによって運営されるべきものと言えます。

　日本の会社法は，外国会社が日本において取引を継続して行うときは，日本における代表者（Q53参照）を定めて登記することを求めていますが，この規定は取引の安全を確保する観点から要請されるものであり，日本における代表者と外国会社の内部関係については，日本の会社法は規定していません。

Chapter Three : コーポレートガバナンス Corporate Governance

Q52 How is a branch of foreign corporation governed?

A The Companies Act does not provide rules which discipline the relationship between a branch office and its head office. Corporate governance of branch office should be governed by the internal rules of the company.

Since a branch office is not an independent legal entity, the profits earned by a branch at the cost of its head office belongs to the same legal entity. There is no need to resolve conflicts between branch and head office by laws. Therefore, the Companies Act does not provide rules which discipline the relationship between branch and head office. Corporate governance of branch office should be governed according to the internal rules of the company.

When a foreign corporation carries out a transaction in Japan, the Companies Act requires the foreign company to appoint and register a representative of Japan (See Q53) in order to protect the safety of transactions. The Companies Act does not stipulate the internal relationship between representatives of Japan and the foreign company.

Q53 日本における代表者とはどういう役職ですか。

A 日本における代表者は，日本における代表権を有しています。

　日本の会社法は，外国会社が日本において取引を継続してしようとするときは，日本における代表者を定め，法務局に登記することを求めています。そして日本代表者のうち，少なくとも1名は日本に住所を有する必要があります。外国会社の日本における代表者は，日本における代表権（**Q45参照**），すなわち日本における業務に関する一切の裁判上または裁判外の行為をする権限が与えられています。この代表権に対して内部的に制限を加えたとしても，善意の第三者には対抗することができません。

Chapter Three : コーポレートガバナンス Corporate Governance

Q53 What is a Representative of Japan?

A A Representative of Japan has the authority to represent the foreign company in Japan.

If a foreign company engages in transactions on a continuous basis in Japan, it is required to appoint a Representative(s) of Japan and register it with the Legal Affairs Bureau. At least one Representative of Japan must have a residential address in Japan. A Representative of Japan has the full authority to represent the foreign company (See Q45) with respect to any and all business activities and court proceedings in Japan. Even if the company puts restrictions on the authority, such limitations are not asserted against a third party without knowledge of such limitation.

141

Chapter 4

ファイナンス
Finance Structure

▶▶ファイナンス

Q54 日本拠点へ事業資金を投下する際に検討すべきポイントは何ですか。

A 一般的に出資または貸付により投資します。選択に際して，ファイナンスの機能のほか，税金も考慮します。

資金調達の方法は，一義的にはファイナンスの機能面から検討されます。一時的な資金不足は短期借入金でカバーされます。レバレッジを高めて株主資本利益率を改善するには借入金を増やします。長期的な安定資金が欲しい場合や，過剰債務を解消するというケースでは増資により調達します。

海外の親会社や関連会社から資金を調達する際には，これに加えて税務面からの検討も重要になります。借入金で調達すると節税が図れることがあります。支払利息は税金計算において費用となるため日本の法人税は減少する一方，貸手の国外関連会社が受け取る利息は税金計算において収益となるため当該地国の法人税が増加します。ここで，日本の税率のほうが高ければ，グループ全体の税負担は減少します。一方増資で調達すると，支払配当は税金の計算上は費用とならず節税効果は生じません。それどころか，株主が配当に対して課税を受けると二重課税が発生します。

借入と増資のどちらを選択するかは企業の自由ですが，節税のために意図的に借入金を増やす行為に対して，課税当局は否定的な姿勢を持っています。そのため日本では，「移転価格税制」「過少資本税制」「過大支払利子税制」の3つの制度によって過度な租税回避行為を防止しています。

Chapter Four : ファイナンス Finance Structure

Q54 What needs to be considered when investing in a business in Japan?

A Generally, a business is financed by debt or equity. Not only the function of each financing but also tax implications should be considered when you decide how to fund.

When you decide how to fund the company, you will primarily consider the function of each financing. Temporary money shortage will be covered by short-term borrowing. If you want to boost the return on equity (ROE) by adding leverage, you will increase debt. If you prefer long-term stable funding, or if a company needs to get out of excessive debt, equity finance will be chosen.

When you raise funds from foreign parent and affiliate companies, tax implications should also be considered. If you choose debt funding, tax may be saved. Since interest expenses are deductible in corporate tax calculation, Japan's corporation income tax decreases, while the interests received by the overseas affiliated company are taxable and the corporate income tax of the lender will be increased. If the tax rate of Japan is higher, the total tax amount of the entire group will decrease. On the other hand, if you raise funds by equity, there will be no tax effect as the dividends will not count as expenses in the tax calculation. Moreover, if the investor is taxed on the received dividends, double taxation will occur.

It is the choice of the company how to finance, but you should know the tax authorities have a negative attitude toward debt financing which may intentionally be arranged instead of equity just for the tax purposes. This is why Japan has three tax avoidance measurements, transfer pricing, thin capitalization rules, and earnings stripping rules.

145

Q55 移転価格税制とはどのような税制ですか。

A 移転価格税制とは，異なる国にあるグループ会社間の取引は，独立企業間価格（市場価格）で行われたものとして課税所得金額を算定する税制です。

　親会社が海外の子会社に製品を販売する際，親会社の国の税率が子会社の国の税率より低いときには，価格を市場価格よりも高めに設定すれば，グループ全体で節税を図ることができます。また，グループ会社間で貸付を行うときに，利率を恣意的に設定することで節税することができます。このように，同じ企業グループに属する会社間の取引では，市場価格とは異なった取引価格を設定し，グループ全体の節税を図ろうとする動機が生じます。

　関連会社間取引の価格が市場価格ではないと税務当局が判断した場合，移転価格税制が発動され，取引価格が独立企業間価格で行われたものとして課税所得金額を算定します。もし課税されれば，国際的な二重課税を引き起こします。移転価格税制により再計算された所得は，すでに一方の関係会社の国で課税されているので，同じ所得に2度課税されることになります。そのため，両国間の相互協議による解決を申し立てることが租税条約によって認められています。

Chapter Four : ファイナンス Finance Structure

Q55 What Is Transfer Pricing Taxation?

A Transfer pricing is a taxation that calculates taxable income by applying the arm's length price — a market price — to international transactions between associated companies.

When the parent company sells products to overseas subsidiaries, if the tax rate of the country of the parent company is lower than that of the country of the subsidiary company, setting the price higher than the market price can save taxes throughout the group. Also, when you arrange international loans between group companies, you can save taxes by arbitrarily setting the interest rate. This way, in intercompany transactions within the same group, there is a motivation to set the transaction price different from the market price to save tax amounts of the entire group.

If the tax authority is not satisfied that the price of an international transaction between associated companies is at the market price, they will apply transfer pricing taxation, calculating taxable income by applying the arm's length price. Transfer pricing taxation results in international double taxation. The income assessed by a country has already been taxed by another country at the level of the other affiliated company; the same income is taxed twice. Taxpayer can apply for the mutual agreement procedure set forth by the applicable tax treaty.

147

Q56 過少資本税制とはどのような税制ですか。

A 過少資本税制は，一定の国外関連者からの借入に関する支払利子の損金算入を制限する税制です。「国外支配株主等」からの借入が自己資本の3倍を超えると，超える部分の金額に対応する利子は損金に算入されません。外国法人の日本支店は，他の損金算入ルールが適用されるため，過少資本税制の適用はありません。

　日本の子会社が海外の親会社から資金を調達する際，日本の税率のほうが高ければ増資より貸付を選択するインセンティブがあるため，日本における租税負担を軽減するために意図的に借入金を選択することが考えられます。このような租税回避行為を封じるため，国外支配株主等から自己資本の3倍を超える借入を行う場合には，それを超える部分の金額に対応する利子を損金に算入しないこととされています。このような税制を過少資本税制といいます。

国外支配株主等とは以下のものをいいます。
- 外国親会社：外国会社で，日本法人の株式を50％以上直接または間接に保有するもの
- 個人支配株主：非居住者で，日本法人の株式を50％以上直接または間接に保有するもの
- 外国兄弟会社：外国会社で，当該外国会社と日本法人が同一の者によって，それぞれその株式の50％以上を直接または間接に保有される関係にあるもの

Chapter Four : ファイナンス Finance Structure

Q56 What is Thin Capitalization Rules?

A Thin capitalization rules restrict the ability of corporations to deduct interest expenses on debt owing to certain related non-residents. Interest deduction will be limited proportionally if a debtor's outstanding debts to "overseas controlling shareholders" exceed 3 times the debtor's equity. The thin-capitalization rules do not apply to Japan branches of foreign corporations, which are subject to different restriction rules.

When a Japan subsidiary raises funds from its overseas parent company, there is an incentive to choose debt funding rather than equity funding if the Japanese tax rate is higher. You may deliberately choose borrowing in order to reduce the tax amount in Japan.

To prevent such tax evasion behavior, companies are not allowed to deduct the excess interest expenses in the tax return if the company borrow from "overseas controlling shareholders" more than three times the equity capital. This is called the thin capitalization rule.

Overseas controlling shareholders are defined as:

- Foreign parent company: A foreign company which directly or indirectly owns 50% or more of the shares of the Japanese corporation
- Individual controlling shareholder: Non-resident who directly or indirectly owns 50% or more of the shares of the Japanese corporation
- Foreign brother company: A foreign company with 50% or more of the shares directly or indirectly owned by the same person who owns 50% or more of the shares in the Japanese corporation

149

外国子会社からの借入金は過少資本税制の規制対象となりません。ただし，過大支払利子税制の課税対象となります（Q57参照）。

Chapter Four : ファイナンス Finance Structure

Debt funding from the foreign subsidiaries are not subject to the Thin Capitalization Rule. Such funding are restricted by the earnings stripping rules (See Q57).

Q57 過大支払利子税制とはどのような税制ですか。

A 一定の国外関連者に対する支払利子が調整所得の50%を超える場合には，その超える部分の金額を損金不算入とする税制です。外国法人の日本支店にも適用されます。

　一定の国外関連者には，外国親会社，個人支配株主，外国兄弟会社のほか，外国子会社も含まれます。外国子会社とは，外国会社で，株式の50％以上を直接または間接に日本法人に保有されているものをいいます。「調整所得」とは，利益の金額に，関連者等に対する支払利子，減価償却費および貸倒損失を加算した金額です。過大支払利子税制と過少資本税制の両方が適用されるときには，損金不算入とする額が大きいほうの制度を適用します。

152

Chapter Four : ファイナンス Finance Structure

Q57　What is Earnings Stripping Rules?

A　Earnings stripping rules limit interest deductions proportionally, if interest expenses paid or payable to certain related non-residents are more than 50% of the adjusted income. The earnings stripping rules also apply to Japan branches of foreign corporations.

Related non-residents include foreign parent companies, individual controlling shareholders, and foreign brother company as well as foreign subsidiaries: A foreign company with 50% or more of the shares directly or indirectly owned by a Japanese company. "Adjusted income" is the sum of profits plus interest payments to related parties, depreciation expenses, and losses on bad debt. If the thin capitalization rules are applicable at the same time, the rules which will deny larger amount of interests are applicable.

153

Q58 国際間の貸付金の利息にはどのような税金がかかりますか。

A 貸手が外国会社の場合，借手である日本法人は利息の支払時に20.42%の源泉税を徴収し納付します。租税条約に基づき税率が軽減されることがあります。貸主である外国会社の本国では，全世界課税を採用している場合には，受取利息は国外所得として課税され，日本で徴収された源泉税は外国税額控除により税額控除が受けられるのが一般的と考えられます。

国内法の源泉税率は20.42%（所得税20％と復興特別所得税0.42%）ですが，本国と日本の間の租税条約で利息に対して限界税率を定めているときには，税率が軽減されます。源泉徴収で完結しますが，日本国内にある恒久的施設を通じて貸し付けている場合には，日本支店の所得として確定申告を行わなければなりません。

本国では，日本からの利息収入は国外所得になりますが，本国の税制が「全世界課税」を採用している場合には国外所得も本国において課税されます。その際，日本で課税された源泉税は，外国税額控除などの二重の課税を排除する措置が図られていることが一般的です。

Chapter Four : ファイナンス Finance Structure

Q58 What taxes will be imposed on interest on international loans?

A If the lender is a foreign corporation, the debting Japanese corporation is required to withhold and pay a 20.42% withholding tax. The tax rate may be reduced by the tax treaty. If the country of the lending corporation adopts world taxation system, foreign interest income will be taxed and the tax amount withheld in Japan will be generally deducted as the foreign tax credit.

Domestic withholding tax rate is 20.42% (Income Tax 20% and Reconstruction Special Income Tax 0.42%). The tax rate will be reduced if the tax treaty between the home country and Japan defines the reduced tax rate on interest. Withholding tax is a final tax unless the loan is made through a permanent establishment (PE) in Japan. PE must file a tax return for the interest income.

Interest income from Japan will be a foreign sourced income in the home country, which is taxable if the home country adopts "World taxation system." It is common that the withholding tax paid in Japan is deducted as a foreign tax credit, to avoid double taxation.

155

Q59　国際間の配当には日本でどのような税金がかかりますか。

A　株主が外国会社の場合，日本法人は配当の支払時に20.42％の源泉税を徴収し納付します。租税条約に基づき税率が軽減されることがあります。株主である外国会社の本国では，全世界課税を採用している場合には，受取配当は国外所得となりますが，海外配当所得を免税としている国は数多くあります。

　株主の配当所得は投資先の国で所得が発生すると考える国際課税の原則があります（OECDモデル条約第10条）。日本の税制も，配当所得は配当を行う会社の所在地で発生したものと考えるため，日本の会社が配当を行う際は源泉税率20.42％（非上場株式：所得税20％と復興特別所得税0.42％）の源泉税が課税されます。本国と日本の間の租税条約で配当に対して限界税率を定めているときには，税率が軽減されます。源泉徴収で完結しますが，日本国内にある恒久的施設を通じて株式を保有している場合には，支店の所得として確定申告を行わなければなりません。

　本国では，日本からの配当収入は国外所得になりますが，本国の税制が「全世界課税」を採用している場合でも，海外配当所得を免税としている国は数多くあります。長らく海外配当所得に対して課税してきたアメリカですが，国外の子会社に滞留していた利益をアメリカ本国に還流させるため，2018年に海外配当所得を免税とする税制改正を行いました。

Chapter Four : ファイナンス Finance Structure

Q59 What taxes will be imposed on international dividends?

A If the shareholder is a foreign corporation, the Japanese corporation is required to withhold and pay a 20.42% withholding tax. The tax rate may be reduced by the tax treaty. If the country of the corporate shareholder adopts world taxation system, dividends will be foreign sourced taxable income. However, many countries exempt tax on overseas dividends.

There is a principle of international taxation, that shareholders' dividend income is deemed income from sources within a country of investee (Article 10 of the OECD Model Convention). Under the Japanese tax law, dividend income is also deemed as income derived from the country of the company distributing dividends. Therefore, a Japanese company is required to deduct and pay 20.42% withholding tax (private company: Income Tax 20% and Reconstruction Special Income Tax 0.42%) on its dividends. The tax rate will be reduced if the tax treaty between the home country and Japan defines the reduced tax rate for dividends. Withholding tax is a final tax unless the foreign shareholder holds the shares through a permanent establishment (PE) in Japan. PE must file a tax return for dividend income.

Dividend income from Japan will be a foreign sourced income in the home country, which is taxable if the home country adopts "World taxation system." However, many countries exempt tax on overseas dividends. The United States had long been taxing overseas dividend income until it introduced the foreign dividends exemption as a part of 2018 tax reform, aiming to return the profits accumulated in foreign subsidiaries back to the United States.

157

Q60 配当の国際二重課税を回避する方法はありますか。

A 外国株主が日本法人からの配当について本国でも課税されると二重課税が発生します。二重課税の対処方法には，一般的に外国税額控除と免税の２つの方法があります。外国税額控除には直接税額控除と間接税額控除の２つの控除方法があります。世界の潮流として多くの国が海外配当を免税としています。

　親会社の所在地国で配当について課税されると，２つの点において二重課税が発生します。１つ目は源泉税による二重課税です。親会社の配当所得に対して，配当を実施した子会社が所在する国（源泉地国）で源泉税が課税されると二重課税が発生します。

　２つ目は利益に対する二重課税です。法人が獲得した利益には，すでに法人税が課税されているにもかかわらず，税引後の利益剰余金から配当を受け取った親会社でさらに課税されると二重課税が生じます。これは，海外配当，国内配当にかかわらず，親子間の配当に課税すると起きる問題です。

　このような二重課税を回避する方法として，①課税するが二重課税について外国で生じた税金は控除する（外国税額控除）方法，②免税として二重課税を排除する方法，の２つの方法があります。外国税額控除のうち，源泉地国で課税された源泉税を控除することを直接税額控除といいます。これに対して，外国子会社が納付した法人税を控除することを間接税額控除といいます。間接税額控除を受けるには，外国法人税額を配当金額に加えて課税所得を算定し（グロスアップ），計算された税額から外国法人税額を控除します。結果として，

158

Chapter Four : ファイナンス Finance Structure

Q60 How to avoid international double taxation on dividends?

A Double taxation will occur if the country of foreign shareholders imposes tax on dividends from Japanese corporations. Generally, there are two ways to cope with double taxation: foreign tax credit and exemption. There are two types of foreign tax credit: direct tax credit and indirect tax deduction. As a world trend, many countries choose to exempt foreign dividends.

If dividends are taxed in the country where the parent company is located, double taxation will occur due to two points. Firstly, it would be taxed twice if withholding tax was imposed in the source country where the subsidiary company is located.

Secondly, tax would be imposed twice on the profits that the company earned. Since corporate income tax has already been imposed on the profits at the level of a subsidiary company, double taxation will arise if dividends, which are distributed from after-tax profits, are further taxed at the parent company level. This is a problem that happens regardless of overseas dividends or domestic dividends.

There are two ways to avoid double taxation: 1) tax, but deduct the tax imposed in a foreign country (foreign tax credit), and 2) just exempt. There are two types of foreign tax credit. Deducting withholding taxes levied in a source country is called "direct foreign tax credit." Deducting the corporate tax paid by a foreign subsidiary is called "indirect foreign tax credit". To take advantage of the indirect foreign tax credit, you will add the foreign income tax to the dividend amounts to obtain the taxable income (gross-up), and deduct the foreign income tax from the computed tax amount. As a result,

159

外国子会社が獲得した利益は本国の法人税率で課税されることになるため，支店の場合と同じ税負担になります。

　海外子会社からの配当を本国でも課税されるとなると，配当を実施しないで海外子会社に利益を留保する，海外に設立した中間持株会社を経由して第三国へ投資するなど，海外所得を本国へ戻さないという弊害が生じます。資金を還流させ本国での投資を促すことを狙って，日本は2009年度の税制改正で間接税額控除の方式から免税方式へ移行しました。米国も2018年に間接税額控除の方式から免税方式へ移行しました。

Chapter Four : ファイナンス Finance Structure

the profits earned by a foreign subsidiary will eventually be taxed at the corporate tax rate of the home country, which is the same result as branches of foreign corporations.

If dividends from overseas subsidiaries are taxable in the home country as well, you may think to hold the profits at the overseas subsidiaries instead of distributing dividends, or invest in third countries via intermediate holding companies established overseas. Japan abolished indirect foreign tax credit and adopted foreign dividends exemption by the 2009 reform in order to encourage companies to retrieve the accumulated profits held by the overseas subsidiaries. The United States also introduced foreign dividends exemption as a part of the 2018 tax reform.

Q61 配当せず留保した場合にどのような税金がかかりますか。

A 一定のプライベートカンパニーは，当期純利益から配当決議額を控除した留保利益が，所得金額の40％など一定の基準値を超えると，「留保金課税」が課せられます。超過した金額に対して，金額に応じて10％～20％の税率で税金が課されます。外国会社の支店には留保金課税の適用はありません。

　日本の個人居住者の配当収入は個人所得税が課せられます。所得に対して法人と個人で二重に課税されることを回避するために，オーナーが強い支配力を持つ会社では配当を行わずに社内に利益を留保することがあります。このような行為を抑止するために，1株主グループの持株割合が50％超である会社は，配当しなかった留保利益から「留保控除額」を差し引いた金額に対して，追加で税金が課税されます。ただし，親会社の株式が1株主グループに50％超を保有されていない子会社には留保金課税は課されません。

　「留保控除額」は次のうち最も多い金額になります。

（1）所得金額の40％

（2）資本金の25％から利益積立金を控除した金額

（3）2,000万円

　税率は，課税対象金額のうち3,000万円以下の部分には10％，3,000万円を超え1億円以下の部分には15％，1億円を超える金額には20％の税率が適用されます。

　資金調達が容易ではない中小企業は，利益を社内に留保する必要性もあるこ

Chapter Four : ファイナンス Finance Structure

Q61 What taxes will be imposed if the company does not distribute earnings as dividends and keep them as retained earnings?

A "Retained earnings tax" will be imposed on certain private companies if the remainder of the net profits after deducting dividends is over a certain threshold such as 40% of taxable income. Excessively retained profits will be taxed at the rate from 10% or 20%. The retained earning tax does not apply to Japanese branches of foreign corporations.

Dividend income earned by individual residents is taxable in Japan. To avoid double taxation on incomes levied at the both level of corporations and individuals, family companies owned by individual owners tend to retain profits within the company instead of paying dividends. To prevent such behavior, additional tax will be imposed on companies which are owned more than 50% by one shareholder group. Taxable amount is the excess amount of the retained profits after deducting the "retaining deduction." However, a subsidiary whose parent company is not owned more than 50% by one shareholder group will be exempted.

"Retaining deduction" is the largest amount among the following:

(1) 40% of taxable income

(2) 25% of capital amount minus the accumulated retained earnings

(3) JPY 20 million

10% tax rate is applied on the first JPY 30 million of taxable amounts, 15% on the next JPY 70 million, and 20% in excess of JPY 100 million.

As it is not easy for small and medium sized companies to raise funds,

163

とから，資本金が１億円以下の会社は留保金課税が適用されません。ただし，株式または持分の100％を大法人（資本金が５億円以上である法人）に保有されている会社は，資本金が１億円以下でも課税されます。これは，規模が大きな同族会社が，留保金課税を逃れるために資本金が１億円以下の子会社を設立して事業を行い子会社に利益を留保することを防止する趣旨です。

留保金課税は外資系企業の日本子会社にも等しく適用されてしまうため，本国の親会社が１株主グループに支配されている資本金５億円以上の会社だと，日本法人の株式を100％保有していれば，日本子会社はその資本金が１億円以下でも留保金課税が適用されます。したがって，留保金課税は外国会社が日本に子会社を設立する際に検討すべき重要なポイントと言えます。

Chapter Four : ファイナンス Finance Structure

SMEs need to retain the profits for their finance. Therefore, SEMs with JPY 100 million or less of capital amount are exempted from the retained earning taxation. However, companies which are 100% owned by a large corporation (companies with JPY 500 million or more of capital amount) will be taxed even if its capital amount is JPY 100 million or less. This prevents tax avoidance behavior of large corporations who set up new small companies to do a business, just because they want to avoid the retained earning tax.

The retained earnings tax is equally applied to a Japanese subsidiary of a foreign company. If the foreign parent company's capital amount is equivalent to JPY 500 million or more, and the parent company is controlled by one shareholder group, the retained earning tax will be imposed on its 100% subsidiary in Japan, even if the capital amount of the subsidiary is JPY 100 million or less. The retained earnings tax is one of the important considerations when a foreign corporation sets up its new subsidiary in Japan.

165

Q62 日本法人の株式または持分を譲渡すると日本でどのような税金がかかりますか。

A 非居住者または外国会社が25％以上保有している本法人の株式または持分を5％以上譲渡するときは，譲渡所得について日本でも課税されます。譲渡者は日本で確定申告を行う必要があります。ただし，日本との租税条約によって免税または軽減されることがあります。そのほか，居住国である本国において，本国の税制に従って課税されることになります。

　出口戦略の一環として投資持分を売却することを検討しておくことは重要です。その際，どのような税金が発生するかは重要な検討ポイントになります。

　まず，国際税務の原則として，株式の譲渡から生じる収益は，株式を所有していた者の居住地で発生するため，投資先国は課税しないものと考えます（OECDモデル条約第13条5項）。

　これに対して，日本の国内法は，少数株主とはいえない株主が一定量の株式を売却する場合は，投資持分ではなく事業の売却にあたると考え，事業資産が存在する日本でも課税します（事業譲渡類似株式）。非居住者または外国会社が株式または持分を25％以上保有している日本法人の株式または持分を5％以上譲渡するときは，株式譲渡所得について日本で課税されます。譲渡者は日本で確定申告を行う必要があります。

　そのほか，日本子会社の総資産の価額の50％以上が不動産である場合，株式譲渡所得は日本でも課税されます（不動産化体株式）。不動産の譲渡益は不動

Chapter Four : ファイナンス Finance Structure

Q62 What taxes will be incurred in Japan when selling shares or equity interests in a Japanese company?

A If a nonresident or a foreign company transfers 5% or more of the shares or equity interests in a corporation which they hold 25% or more of the shares or equity interests, capital gain is taxable in Japan as well. The seller is required to file a tax return in Japan. However, tax exemption or reduction may be granted by the tax treaty with Japan. Besides, the capital gain will be taxed according to the tax system of the home country.

It is important to consider how to sell your investment as part of the exit strategy. Tax implications are always one of key factors.

There is a principle of international taxation that capital gain derived from selling shares occurs in the place of residence of the owner, and that the investee country will not tax (Article 13.5 of the OECD Model Convention).

On the other hand, according to Japan's domestic law, when shareholders, who are not minority shareholders, sell out a big number of shares, it is considered that they sold the business, not the investment amount. Therefore, capital gain is taxed in Japan, where the business assets have been existing ("Business transferring transaction"). Capital gain will be taxed if a non-resident or a foreign company transfers 5% or more of the shares or equity interests in a Japanese corporation with 25% or more of the shares or equity interests held by the seller. The seller is required to file a tax return in Japan.

Capital gain is also taxed on sales transactions of shares or equity interests in a Japanese company which owns real estate with a value of

167

産の所在地国でも課税されますが，法人に不動産を所有させ株式または持分を売却することで課税を逃れようとする課税回避行為を防止するために，不動産化体株式の譲渡益は法人の所在地で課税されます。

　以上は，日本の国内法による取扱いですが，本国と日本の間の租税条約で株式譲渡益について別の定めがあるときには条約が優先します。例えば，日米租税条約では，不動産化体株式は日本国内法とほぼ同様の規定を置いていますが，事業譲渡類似株式の規定はなく，「その他譲渡所得」の規定に基づき，居住地国，すなわち株主の所在地国にのみ課税権が認められています。そのため日本子会社の株式譲渡は日本では課税されません。

　これに対して，日本シンガポール租税条約では，不動産化体株式，事業譲渡類似株式ともに，日本国内法とほぼ同様の規定を置いています。したがって，シンガポールの親会社が日本子会社の株式を5％以上売却する際には，日本で課税されます。

Chapter Four : ファイナンス Finance Structure

more than half of the total assets of the company ("Real estate transferring transaction"). Gains on transferring real estates are taxed in the country where the real estate exists. In order to prevent tax avoidance behavior trying to escape taxation by letting a company own real estates and selling its shares, gains from real estate transferring transaction are taxed in the place where the corporation exists.

If the tax treaty with Japan have provisions which treat differently from the Japanese domestic treatments above, the treaty takes precedence. For example, the Japan - US Tax Treaty provides the same treatment for Real estate transferring transaction while there is no provision for Business transferring transaction, treating as "other capital gain" that is only taxed in the country of residence. Therefore, gains on transfer of shares in Japanese subsidiaries are not taxed in Japan.

On the other hand, the Japan - Singapore Tax Treaty has the same provisions as those of the Japanese domestic law, for both Real estate transferring transaction and Business transferring transaction. Therefore, when the parent company in Singapore sells the shares of the Japanese subsidiary by 5% or more, capital gain is taxed in Japan.

169

▶▶株式会社のファイナンス

> **Q63　借入金で資金を調達するにはどのような手続が必要になりますか。**

A　取締役会を設置している会社では，多額の借入金を行うには取締役会の決議が必要になります。取締役会を設置していない会社では，取締役の過半数の合意は不要です。

　取締役会を設置している会社では，原則として業務執行の決定は取締役会の決議が必要です。法定で定められている重要事項以外は各取締役に委任できますが，重要事項に「多額の借財」が含まれているため，会社にとって多額といえる借入金を行うには，取締役会の決議が必要になります。

　取締役会を設置していない会社では，原則として業務執行の決定は個々の取締役が決定します。法定で定められている重要事項の決定は取締役の過半数の合意が必要とされていますが，重要事項に「多額の借財」は含まれていないことから，取締役の過半数の合意は不要です。

Chapter Four : ファイナンス Finance Structure

Q63 What procedures are required for debt financing?

A For Company with Board of Directors to make a large amount of borrowing, a resolution of the board of directors is required, while it is not necessary to make an agreement with a majority of directors of Company with Board of Directors.

Basically, resolutions of the board of directors are required for Company with Board of Directors to make decisions on business. Decision making power can be delegated to each director, except for important matters such as "borrowing a large amount of money".

On the other hand, each director of Company with Board of Directors has decision making power. An agreement with a majority of the directors are required to make decisions on important matters stipulated by Companies Act, which does not include "borrowing a large amount of money."

171

Q64 新株を発行して増資するにはどのような手続が必要になりますか。

A 株式譲渡制限会社は，原則として株主総会の特別決議により決定します。公開会社は，機動的な資金調達が必要になることもあるため，取締役会の決議で新株の発行を行えます。定款で定めた発行可能株式総数を超える新株発行を行うには，株主総会の特別決議により定款を変更する必要があります。

　新株を発行して増資するには株主割当増資，第三者割当増資，および公募増資の3つの方法があります。現在の株主全員に対して持株数に応じて新株を発行することを株主割当増資といいます。第三者や特定の株主に新株を発行することを第三者割当増資といいます。株式市場を通じて広く一般の投資家を対象に株主を募集し新株を発行することを公募増資といいます。

　現在の株主以外に株式を発行すると既存株主の持株比率が低下してしまいます。また，発行価格が時価を下回ると既存株主の株式価値が下がってしまいます。このような問題を株式の希薄化（dilution）といいます。株式の希薄化を緩和する観点から一定の制限が設けられています。

　まず，会社が発行できる株式数の上限（発行可能株式総数）を定款で定め，それを超える新株発行を行う際には，株主総会の特別決議による定款変更が必要となる仕組にしています。株主は事前にどこまで持株比率が低下する可能性があるかを予見することができます。

　また，公開会社が，会社の支配株主が変更となるような新株発行を行う際には，既存株主に一定の保護を与えています。具体的には，事前の通知または公

Chapter Four : ファイナンス Finance Structure

Q64 What procedures are required to issue new shares for equity funding?

A A private company needs to make a special resolution at the general meeting of shareholders while a public company can issue with a resolution by the board of directors to secure a flexible funding. If you issue new shares exceeding the authorized shares, it is necessary to change the articles of incorporation with a special resolution at the general meeting of shareholders.

There are three ways to issue new shares: Shareholder allotment, Third-party allotment, and Public offering. Shareholder allotment offers new shares to all the existing shareholders on pro rata basis. Third-party allotment offers to third parties or specific shareholders. Public offering offers to the public through stock exchange markets.

When a company issues new shares to others than existing shareholders, it will reduce their existing proportional ownership of that company. If the issuing price is less than the market price, it can reduce the value of their existing shares. This problem is called dilution. There are certain restrictions on the procedures of issueing new shares in order to ease share dilution.

Firstly, the limit on the number of shares that a company can issue is set forth in the articles of incorporation. This is known as the number of authorized shares. If you issue new shares exceeding the number of authorized shares, it is necessary to change the articles of incorporation, which requires a special resolution at shareholders' meeting. Shareholders can foresee how much their shares could be diluted in the future.

Secondly, if a Public Company decides to issue shares that would change the controlling shareholders of the company, existing shareholders are

173

告により既存株主に反対する機会を与え，議決権の10％以上を有する株主が反対を表明する場合には，株主総会の普通決議による承認を受けなければならないとされています（会社法206条の2）。

　既存株主の株式の経済的価値を保護する観点から，市場価格と比べて特に有利な価額で新株を発行するときには，株主総会の特別決議による承認を受けなければなりません。株主割当以外の方法で新株発行を行うと，既存株主の持株比率に希薄化が生じますが，新株が時価で発行される限り株式の経済的価値は維持されます。

Chapter Four : ファイナンス Finance Structure

provided with some protections. Existing shareholders are given opportunities by prior notice for them to express opposition. If shareholders who hold 10% or more of voting rights oppose to issuing new shares, ordinary resolution of shareholders' meeting is required for approval (the Companies Act Article 206-2)

To protect the economic value of shares of existing shareholders, approval by a special resolution of the general meeting of shareholders is required when the company issues new shares at a price lower than the market price. Although Third-party allotment and Public offering cause dilution on existing shareholders' ownership, economic value of the shares can be maintained as long as new shares are issued at the market price.

Q65 赤字であっても配当することはできますか。

A 当期決算が赤字であっても利益剰余金の配当可能残高があれば配当することができます。

　株式会社は株主有限責任制度（Q4参照）を採用しているため，会社債権者への弁済の原資は会社の資産しかありません。もし，株主に対して無制限に配当できるとなると，過度な配当により支払不能に陥ったとしても，債権者は株主有限責任制度で保護されている株主に対して請求することができません。このような株主有限責任制度の悪用を防ぐために，配当は利益剰余金の範囲でしか行うことができません。

　実際には，利益剰余金のすべてを配当できるわけではありません。債権者を保護する観点から，投資有価証券の含み益，繰延資産，のれん，自己株式を控除する必要があります。また，最低資本金制度がないことから資本金が1円のような会社も存在しますが，そのような会社の債権者を保護するために純資産が300万円以上でなければ配当できないこととされています（会社法458条）。

　配当は，原則として，株主総会の普通決議によって決定します。ただし，会計監査人（Q48参照）を設置している会社など一定のガバナンスを構築している場合には，取締役会が決議する旨を定款で定めることができます（会社法459条）。

Chapter Four : ファイナンス Finance Structure

Q65 Is a company allowed to distribute dividends when the company made losses?

A If there is a distributable balance of retained earnings, the company can make dividend payments even if it made losses for the current year.

As K.K. adopts the shareholders limited liability (See Q4), creditors can only rely on the company's assets for the payments. If a company is allowed to distribute dividends freely, shareholders may demand so much dividends that the company becomes insolvent to creditors, who cannot claim shareholders under the shareholders limited liability. In order to prevent misuse of the limited liability, dividends can only be made within retained earnings.

In fact, not all the amount of retained earnings can be distributed. From the viewpoint of protecting creditors, it is required to deduct unrealized gains on investment securities, deferred assets, goodwill, and treasury shares. Besides, to protect creditors of companies with small capital amount like a company with 1-yen capital, a company is required to have net assets at least JPY 3 million when it makes dividend payments (the Companies Act Article 458).

As a general rule, dividends will be determined by an ordinary resolution of the shareholders' meeting. However, if you have established certain governance such as companies with statutory external auditor (See Q48), dividends can be determined by the board of directors if you state so in the articles of incorporation (the Companies Act Article 459).

Q66 株式を譲渡するにはどのような手続が必要になりますか。

A 株式は原則として自由に譲渡できますが，譲渡が制限されている株式の場合は，会社の承諾を得る必要があります。

投資の元本を会社から回収することが原則として認められていない株式会社において，株主が株式を譲渡する権利を持つことは株式会社の重要な原則の1つとなっています。一方で，家族経営企業などの中小企業では，株主は見知らぬ者が株主となることを望まないこともあります。そこで，株式の全部または一部について，株式を譲渡する際に会社の承諾を必要とする制限を設けることができます。すべての株式について譲渡を制限している会社を株式譲渡制限会社（プライベートカンパニー），それ以外を公開会社（パブリックカンパニー）といい，登記簿で確認することができます。

譲渡の承認は取締役会が行いますが（取締役会非設置会社は株主総会），定款の定めにより株主総会や代表取締役など他の機関に承認権限を与えることも可能です。

会社は承認請求日から2週間以内に決定内容を通知しなければならず，通知がなければ承認されたものとみなされます。譲渡の承認が得られない場合には，会社を含む他の者を買取人に指定するよう請求することができます。

承認なく譲渡された株式について，会社は株主名簿の変更に応じる必要はなく，譲受人は議決権や配当請求権など株主権を行使することができません。

Chapter Four : ファイナンス Finance Structure

Q66 What procedures are required when I sell shares?

A As a basic principle, shares can be freely transferred. If your shares are transfer-restricted, it is necessary to obtain consent from the company.

It is one of the important principles of K.K. that shareholders have the right to sell shares in K.K., because K.K. is basically not allowed to refund the investment amount to shareholders. On the other hand, shareholders in SMEs such as family-owned companies may not want unknown people to become shareholders. Therefore, you can put a restriction on all or certain shares that requires shareholders to obtain the company's consent when selling. Companies that put restrictions on all of their shares are called Private Companies, and companies that don't are called Public Companies. You can identify the type from the company register.

The board of directors will approve the transfer (Company without Board of Directors requires an approval of shareholders' meeting). It is possible to grant approval authority to other organizations such as general shareholders' meeting or representative directors if you state so in the articles of incorporation.

The company must notify the conclusion within two weeks from the date of request, otherwise it is deemed to have approved. If the company refuses to give approval of transfer, you can request the company to appoint another buyer of the shares. The company can be the buyer.

If shares have been transferred without approval, the company does not have to change the owner's name in its register of shareholders. Which means that the transferee cannot exercise shareholder rights such as voting and receiving dividends.

179

Q67　会社が株主から株式を取得することはできますか。

A　購入価額が配当可能利益（Q65参照）の範囲内であれば，株式譲渡制限会社は株主総会の特別決議によって自己株式を取得することができます。ただし，株主平等の原則より，他の株主は自己も売主に加えるよう請求することができます。

　会社が発行した株式を自ら買い取ることは，株主に対して持分を払い戻すことと同じ経済効果をもたらします。株式会社は，出資者の有限責任制度（Q4参照）を採用しているため，原則として株主に対して投資元本を返還することが認められていません。ただし，配当可能利益（Q65参照）の範囲であれば，会社が株主から株式を取得することが認められています。特定の株主から自己株式を取得するには，株主総会の特別決議が必要です。その場合，その株主は利害関係者であるため，議決権を行使することができません（会社法160条4項）。

　換金困難な非上場株式について売却機会の平等を図るため，他の株主は自己も売主に加えるよう請求することができます（会社法160条3項）。会社は株主総会の前に他の株主に対して，売主追加請求権を行使できることを通知しなければなりません（会社法160条2項）。定款に売主追加請求権を他の株主に与えないと定めることは可能ですが，この定款変更には株主全員の同意が必要です（会社法164条）。

　なお，譲渡制限株式の譲渡承認を拒否して会社が買取る場合（Q66参照）には，他の株主に売主追加請求権は発生しません（会社法162条）。

Chapter Four : ファイナンス Finance Structure

Q67 Can a company buy back shares from shareholders?

A A private company will be permitted by a special resolution of shareholders' meeting to buy back shares from shareholders, as long as the purchase amount is within distributable earnings (See Q65). As a principle of equal treatment of shareholders, other shareholders will have the right to request the company to buy back their shares as well.

Purchasing shares by the issuing company has the same economic effect as refunding shares to the shareholders. Since K.K. adopts the limited liability (See Q4), it is not allowed to refund the principal of investment to the shareholders, which is a basic principle of K.K. However, a company will be permitted to buy back shares from shareholders if the company has distributable retained earnings (See Q65). A special resolution of the general meeting of shareholders is required to buy treasury stock from certain shareholders, where such shareholders are not allowed to exercise voting rights (the Companies Act Article 160 (4)).

In order to provide equal opportunities for shareholders to sell unlisted shares, which are difficult to sell, other shareholders will have the right to request the company to buy back their shares (the Companies Act Article 160 (3)). The company must inform other shareholders before the general meeting that they can exercise the right to claim for buy-back (the Companies Act Article 160 (2)). It is possible to declare in the articles of incorporation, that shareholders will not have the right to claim for buy-back. You need to have an agreement of all shareholders when you add this clause in the articles of incorporation (the Companies Act Article 164).

If the company buys from shareholders who applied for transfer approval (See Q66) and was refused, the other shareholders will not have the right to claim for buy-back (the Companies Act Article 162).

181

Q68 会社に対して株式を譲渡するとどのような税金がかかりますか。

A 譲渡価額を投資元本相当額と利益配当相当額に区分し，投資元本相当額は，取得価額との差額が譲渡損益として取り扱われ，利益配当相当額は，配当として課税されます。

投資元本相当額とは，投資元本の返還にあたるものとして計算された金額です。貸借対照表の資本金と資本積立金の合計額のうち当該株式に対応する部分として計算します。投資元本相当額と取得価額の差額は，譲渡損益として取り扱われます。利益配当相当額は，会社に留保されてきた累積利益の返還にあたるものとして，配当として課税されます。

なお，株主が日本の居住者の場合，譲渡益に対する税率は20％の固定税率ですが，配当所得は累進税率の適用を受けます。株主が日本の内国法人の場合，子会社からの配当金は益金不算入になり，譲渡損益は益金または損金に算入されます。

ところで，買収により子会社化した会社に直ちに自己株式を取得させると，一般的に株式取得価額は投資元本相当額より高い金額となっていることから譲渡損失が発生する一方，利益配当相当額は益金不算入となるので，意図的に節税機会を作り出すことができます。このスキームを使って多額の節税を行った企業の税務訴訟（日本IBM事件）で課税当局が敗訴したことから，このスキームを封じるために次のルールが設けられています。

- 株式を100％保有する親会社から自己株式を取得する場合，株式譲渡損益は計上されない
- 自己株式として取得されることを予定して取得した株式については，自己株式として取得された際に生ずるみなし配当については，益金不算入制度が適用されない

Chapter Four : ファイナンス Finance Structure

Q68 What taxes will be imposed if I sell my shares to the company?

A Selling price is divided into two parts: principal and deemed dividend. The difference between principal part and purchase cost is treated as capital gain/loss. Deemed dividend is treated as dividend income.

Principal part is an amount that is calculated as a return of investment principal, which is calculated proportionally to the total amount of capital amount and capital reserve on the balance sheet. The difference between principal part and purchase cost is treated as capital gain/loss. Dividend part is deemed as a return of accumulated earnings that have been retained in the company, which is taxed as dividends.

If the selling shareholder is an individual resident in Japan, the tax rate on the capital gain is a fixed rate of 20%, while dividend income is taxed by progressive rate. If the shareholder is a domestic corporation in Japan, a dividend from the subsidiary will be tax-exempt, while capital gain will be taxable in corporate tax calculation.

A tax avoidance opportunity would be created if a company acquires another company and lets it buy back the shares immediately. Since the purchase cost of the shares that the company acquired is normally higher than the principal part of the acquired subsidiary, the company would recognize a capital loss, while dividends income from a subsidiary are not taxable. The following rules were introduced to prevent tax avoidance behaviors, after the tax authority has lost at the court in the case of IBM Japan where IBM reduced a numerous tax amount by using this tax scheme.

- Capital loss is not recognized if a company buys back shares from 100% parent company
- Tax exemption is not applied on deemed dividends of the shares which have been acquired with the intention to buy-back after acquisition

183

▶▶合同会社のファイナンス

Q69　新たな出資者を追加して資金調達するにはどのような手続が必要になりますか。

A　原則として社員全員の同意が必要ですが，多数決で変更できると定款で定めることも可能です。

　合同会社は，少数の出資者が緊密に協業して自ら事業経営にあたる会社です。そのため，新たに出資者を追加するためには原則として社員全員の同意が必要です。出資者である社員は定款に記載されるため，新たに出資者を加えるには定款の変更が必要になります。定款の変更は原則として社員全員の同意が必要ですが，定款の変更方法について，例えば社員の過半数で定款を変更できる，というように定款で定めることができます。

Chapter Four : ファイナンス Finance Structure

Q69 What procedures are required to add a new member and inject new money?

A The consent of all existing members is required to add a new member. However, you can state in the article of incorporation that the majority of votes will be enough.

G.K. is a company with a small number of members who work closely with each other to manage the business by themselves. In this sense, all existing members must agree when adding a new member. Since members are stated in the articles of incorporation, it is necessary to modify the articles of incorporation in order to add new investors. The articles of incorporation can be modified with the consent of all members. However, you may choose to state in the article of incorporation, that an agreement from the majority of members will be enough to modify the articles of incorporation.

185

Q70 合同会社の配当はどのように行われますか。

A 毎年の利益を「損益分配の割合」に基づいて各社員に計算上分配することで各社員の持分を増加させておき，各社員は必要に応じて合同会社に対して自分の持分から配当するよう請求します。

　合同会社には分配という概念があります。毎年の利益を「損益分配の割合」に基づいて各社員に計算上分配し，各社員の持分を増加させます。そして社員は，合同会社に対して自分の持分から配当するよう請求することができます。

　合同会社は少数の社員で経営する閉鎖的な会社なので，「損益分配の割合」は定款で自由に定めることができます。例えば，定款には「総社員の協議により決定する」と定めておき，事業年度ごとに社員の貢献度を全社員で評価して利益を分配することが考えられます。損益分配の割合について定款に定めがないときは，株式会社のように各社員の出資額に応じて分配されます。

Chapter Four : ファイナンス Finance Structure

Q70 How does G.K. distribute dividends?

A G.K. allots current year's profits to the equity account of each member based on the "proportion of profit and loss allocation". Then, each member will individually request the company to pay dividends from their equity account anytime they want.

G.K. has the concept of allocation, which K.K. does not have. G.K. calculates each member's portion of the current year's profits based on the "proportion of profit and loss allocation", and add it to the equity account of each member. Then, each member will individually request the company to pay dividends from their equity account anytime they want.

Since G.K. is a closed company which is operated by a small number of members, the "proportion of profit and loss allocation" can be freely determined in the articles of incorporation. For example, it is allowed that the articles of incorporation prescribe "profits shall be allocated by discussion of all members", by which the members evaluate the contribution of each member to allot the profits every year. If the articles of incorporation have no provision, profits are allocated, proportionally to the investment amount in the same way as K.K.

187

Q71　持分の譲渡はどのような手続が必要になりますか。

A　原則として他の社員全員の承諾が必要ですが，定款によって自由に承認方法を変えることが可能です。承諾を要しないと定款で定めることも可能です。

　原則として他の社員全員の承諾が必要です。業務を執行しない社員の持分は，業務執行社員の全員の承諾が必要です。これら承諾方法について，定款によって別の方法を定めることが可能です。定款の定め方については特に制限がないため，例えば，承諾を要しないとすることも可能です。

Chapter Four : ファイナンス Finance Structure

Q71 What procedures will be required for selling equity in G.K.?

A The agreement of all the existing members is necessary to sell the equity. It is possible to change the way of agreement by describing it in the articles of incorporation. You may even state that no consent is required.

Transfer of equity needs to be approved with the agreement from all members. Equity of the non-executive members only requires agreement from all executive members. It is possible to decide other ways to approve by describing it in the articles of incorporation. There are no particular restrictions on changing the way of agreement. It is allowed to set forth in the articles of incorporation that no consent is required.

189

Q72 社員は出資金の一部を払い戻すことはできますか。

A 合同会社は，出資者の有限責任制度（Q5参照）を採用していますが，定款に記載されている出資額を変更することで，個々の社員は自らの出資元本を払い戻すことが認められています。

資本剰余金は，債権者の保護手続を経ることなく払い戻すことが認められています。資本金は，資本剰余金では財源が不足する場合に限って払戻しを行うことができますが（会社法626条2項），その際には債権者保護手続が必要です。公告および催告の手続を行い，債権者が異議を申し立てた場合には，債務を弁済するまたは担保を提供する必要があります（会社法627条）。

なお，社員の出資金のうち資本金に組み入れる金額は，自由に決定することができます（会社計算規則44条2項）。例えば，資本金をゼロとし，全額を資本剰余金としておくことも可能です。

社員が破産するなどして合同会社の持分が債権者に差し押えられた場合，債権者が代位権に基づき払戻請求権を行使する可能性があります。そのような事態に備えて，そもそも社員に対して払戻請求権を認めないと定款に記載することも可能です（会社法624条2項）。

Chapter Four : ファイナンス Finance Structure

Q72 Can members claim a refund of their investment amount in G.K.?

A Although G.K. adopts the limited liability (See Q5), it is allowed to refund investment amount to members by rewriting their investment amount in the articles of incorporation.

Capital reserve can be refunded without any creditors' protection procedures. Capital amount can be refunded only when the capital reserve is insufficient for refund (the Companies Act Article 626 (2)), which requires the company to take creditor protection procedures. The company notifies its creditors through public announcement and individual notification. If creditors raise objections to the refund from capital amount, the company is obliged to make payments to the creditors or provide collateral (the Companies Act Article 627).

There are no rules on how much amount should be allotted to capital amount when members invest into G.K. (Accounting Article 44 (2)). You can even allot all the investment amount into capital reserve with zero capital amount.

In the case that a member goes bankrupt and the equity amount in G.K. is seized, the creditor may exercise the right to request refund based on the subrogation right. To prevent such a situation, you may state in the articles of incorporation that the right to claim refund is not given to the members. (the Companies Act Article 624 (2)).

191

Q73 社員を辞めて持分全額を払い戻すことはできますか。

A 6カ月前までに予告することで，事業年度の終了時において退社することができます。退社した社員は，その持分の払戻しを請求することができます。

　社員の持分は，投資元本と累積利益で構成されています。そのため，退社する社員に持分を払い戻すとなると，投資額のうち資本金に組み入れていた額も払い出すことになるため，債権者保護手続を取る必要があります（Q72参照）。これに対して，資本金を減少させないで払戻しを行うことも可能です。その場合，他の社員に帰属している資本剰余金または利益剰余金を原資として払い戻し，その分だけ他の社員に帰属する持分のうち資本金の割合が増加することになります。

　社員の退社について，やむを得ない事情があるとき，または，すべての社員が同意する場合（定款で要件を変更することは可能）には，予告期間なく，いつでも退社することができます。

　社員の持分を差し押さえた債権者は，6カ月前までに予告することで，社員を強制的に退社させ，払戻しを請求することができます。

Chapter Four : ファイナンス Finance Structure

Q73 Can I quit being a member of G.K. and claim a refund of the full amount of equity?

A Members can leave the company at the end of the business year by giving 6-month prior notice. The member can request a refund of the full amount of equity in G.K.

As a member's equity is comprised of the investment principal and cumulative profits, some portion of capital amount must be paid back when a member leaves the company and gets a refund. Therefore, the creditor protection procedures (See Q72) are required. However, it is possible to make a refund without reducing the capital amount. In that case, the company will reduce capital reserve or retained earnings which belongs to other members. Other members will take on more portion of capital amount.

You are allowed to resign the membership at any time without prior notice, if you have to leave the company due to unavoidable circumstances or when all employees agree (it is possible to change the way of agreement by stating it in the articles of incorporation).

A creditor who seized a member's equity can force the member to resign and request a refund, by notifying six months in advance.

193

▶▶支店のファイナンス

Q74 支店が本店から資金の供給を受ける際に検討すべきポイントは何ですか。

A 本店に対する支払利息は，移転価格税制および過大支払利子税制の規制対象となるほか，「PE帰属資本に対応する負債利子の損金不算入」により損金算入が制限されるので留意が必要です。

内部取引である支払利息は，税金目的で不当に調整される可能性があることから，移転価格税制（Q55参照）が及び，過大支払利子税制（Q57参照）が適用されます。

さらに，「PE帰属資本に対応する負債利子の損金不算入」によって損金算入が制限されます。これは，支店が本店から分離独立した独立企業であると仮定し，自己資本の額をみなし計算によって算定し，実際の本店勘定がその額に満たない場合には，本来は出資として調達されるべき資金が借入として計上されているものとみなして，その過大とみなした部分について支払利子の損金算入を否認するという制度です。この制度と重複することから，過少資本税制（Q56参照）は支店に適用されません。

194

Chapter Four : ファイナンス Finance Structure

Q74 What needs to be considered when a branch office is financed by the head office?

A Interest expenses payable to the head office are subject to transfer pricing, earnings stripping rules, and "Limiting interest deductions corresponding to PE attributable capital"

Transfer Pricing (See Q55) and earnings stripping rules(See Q57) will apply to internal transactions including interest payments from a branch to a head office, because it is possible for the profits of a branch to be unduly transferred to the head office by freely adjusting.

Besides, "Limiting interest deductions corresponding to PE attributable capital" is applied. Under this rule, branches are required to calculate its deemed equity amount as if the branch were an independent entity from headquarters. If the actual head-office account is less than that, there is deemed excessive borrowings from the head office, and interests on such excessive borrowings are not allowed to be deducted against profits.

Thin capitalization rules (See Q56) do not apply to branches since they overlap with this limitation.

195

設立手続
Incorporation

▶▶株式会社

Q75　最低株主数および最低資本金の規制はありますか。

A　株式会社の設立準拠法である会社法は，株主数および資本金に制限を設けていません。そのため，株主1名，資本金1円の株式会社を設立することができます。ただし，駐在員の在留資格（ビザ）などその他の法令や規制によって一定の資本金が必要になることがあるので留意が必要です。また，資本金の登記において認められている通貨は日本円のみです。

　本国本社や関連会社から日本法人に転勤で駐在員を派遣する場合には，「企業内転勤」というカテゴリーの在留資格を取得することが一般的ですが，外国人が日本で事業を行うために株式会社を設立し，取締役として事業を経営するために日本に滞在するには「経営・管理」というカテゴリーの在留資格が必要になります。その場合，事業の規模として2人以上の常勤職員または資本金が500万円以上であることが要件の1つとなっています。

　資本金の通貨は円しか認められていません。商業登記において資本金は登記事項となっており，日本円での登記しか認められていないからです。

Chapter five : 設立手続 Incorporation

Q75 Are there minimum requirements for the capital amount and the number of shareholders?

A The Companies Act, the law governing incorporation of K.K., has no requirements for the capital amount and the number of shareholders. So, you can set up a company with a capital of JPY 1 and one shareholder. However, you may be required a certain amount for the capital by other laws and regulations such as the status of residence (Visa) for expatriates. Japanese yen is the only currency allowed for capital registration.

When a parent company or an affiliated company transfers their employees to Japan as expatriates, they generally choose "Intra-company Transferee" status visa. In the case that an individual foreigner incorporates K.K. and moves to Japan to conduct business as a director of the new company, the director needs to apply for "Investor/Business Manager" status visa, which requires the company to have at least either 2 full-time employees or 5 million yen of the capital amount.

Only Japanese yen is allowed as the capital currency. This is because the capital amount is required to be registered in commercial registration, which only allows registration in Japanese yen.

199

Q76　株式会社の設立の流れについて教えてください。

A　4つのステップがあります。まず，株主となる予定の者が発起人となり，定款を作成して公証人の認証を受けます。次に，発起人は，株式を引き受けて出資を履行して株主になります。その後，会社を経営する取締役が選任され，最後に法務局に対して代表権を持つ取締役が設立登記の申請を行います。

ステップ1：定款の作成

　定款には，紙で作成した定款と，電子定款の2種類があります。電子定款はPDFファイルに電子署名したものをいいます。紙で作成した定款には印紙税が4万円かかりますが，電子定款は印紙税が免除されるため，電子定款のほうが一般的です。定款の署名は発起人が行いますが，発起人が会社などの法人である場合，法人から権限を与えられた自然人が署名します。電子定款の場合，当局が受入れ可能な電子署名を外国人が作成するのは困難なため，司法書士や公認会計士に電子定款の作成を委任します。

　定款は公証人の認証を受ける必要があります。定款の認証料は5万円です。外国会社が発起人となる場合，その国の公証権限ある官公署が作成した法人資格証明書，その外国会社の代表者の署名証明書を公証人に対して提示しなければなりません。なお，公証人の認証が要求されるのは設立時の原資定款のみであり，設立後の定款の変更について認証を受ける必要はありません。

Chapter five : 設立手続 Incorporation

Q76 What are the steps to incorporating K.K.?

A Incorporating K.K. is a four-step process. 1) a person(s) who wishes to become a shareholder is appointed as an incorporator(s) called "hokkinin", and prepares the articles of incorporation and gets it notarized by a Japanese notary public. 2) the incorporator(s) subscribes shares and contributes to the company to become a shareholder. 3) a director(s) who operates the company is appointed. 4) a director(s) who has representation authority applies for registration of incorporation with the Legal Affairs Bureau.

Step1: Completing articles of incorporation

Two types of articles of incorporation are available: paper-based and electronic-based. Electronic articles of incorporation are PDF files with digital signatures. Electronic articles are popular because they are exempted from the stamp duty, which costs JPY 40,000 if you choose paper-based articles. Your articles of incorporation will need to be signed by the incorporator(s). If the incorporator is a company or other incorporated body, the articles must be signed by an individual authorized by that body. It is difficult for foreigners to make an electronic signature acceptable by the authority. In such cases, they usually appoint a qualified person like judicial scrivener and CPA as their attorney-in-fact to prepare the electronic article of incorporation.

Articles of incorporation must be checked and notarized by a notary public registered in Japan. Notarization fee is JPY 50,000. In the case that a foreign corporation becomes an incorporator, the notary public requires a corporation registration of the company issued by a public office with notary authority, and a signature certificate of a representative of the company.

201

ステップ2：出資の履行

　次に，発起人は，株式を引き受けて出資を履行して株主になります。出資額が全額支払われたことを証明するため，引受人から払込があった銀行口座の通帳の写しを法務局に提出します。預金の口座名義人は発起人でなければなりません。預金口座は，①日本の銀行の国内本支店，②日本の銀行の海外支店，③外国銀行の日本国内支店，のいずれかの預金口座でなければなりません。

　発起人が外国会社の場合，これらの預金口座を保有していることはまれです。そのため，発起人ではなく，設立時取締役名義の口座でも良いとされています。発起人および設立時取締役の全員が日本国内に住所を有していない場合，要件を満たす口座を保有していないことがあります。その場合に限り，特例として，発起人および設立時取締役以外の者（自然人に限られず，法人も含みます）の預金口座も認められるようになりました（平成29年3月17日民商第41号通達）。実務では，設立業務を依頼している日本国内の会計事務所などの預金口座を利用します。

ステップ3：取締役の選任

　発起人は，出資の履行が完了した後，設立時取締役を選任します。設立時取締役は設立手続が法令・定款に違反していないかを調査し報告しなければなりません。

ステップ4：設立登記

　最後に，法務局に対して代表権を持つ取締役が設立登記の申請を行います。

Chapter five : 設立手続 Incorporation

Note that only initial articles of incorporation are required to be notarized. Amendments of the articles of incorporation don't need notarization.

Step2: Contribution

The incorporator(s) will subscribe shares and make contributes to the company to become a shareholder. To prove that the full amount of investment has been paid, it is required to submit to the Legal Affairs Bureau a copy of the bank statements of the bank account that received contributions from the subscriber(s). The owner of the bank account must be an incorporator. The bank account must be opened at ① head and branch offices of a Japanese bank, ② overseas branches of a Japanese bank, or ③ Japan branches of a foreign bank.

If a foreign corporation is the incorporator, it is rare to have a bank account in those branches. The authority allows use of a bank account owned by a proposed representative director of the new company. In the case that none of the incorporators and directors live in Japan, it is quite rare for them to have a qualified bank account. Only in that case, the authority started to accept bank accounts of persons (including corporations) other than incorporators and directors of the company (Circular 41, Mar 17, 2017). In practice, a bank account of the accounting firm which provides incorporation services is used as a part of the incorporation services.

Step3: Appoint directors

After completing the contribution, the incorporator(s) will appoint a director(s). The director(s) must report the results of the investigation on whether incorporation procedures are in compliance with laws and regulations, as well as articles of incorporation.

Step4: Registration

Finally, a director who has the representation authority applies for

203

定款，払込み証明書のほか，取締役の就任承諾書などの必要書類を添えて申請します。弁護士，司法書士および公認会計士による代理申請が認められています。申請時に納付する登録免許税は，資本金の0.7％と15万円のいずれか高いほうとされています。

Chapter five：設立手続 Incorporation

registration of establishment with the Legal Affairs Bureau, submitting articles of incorporation, a copy of bank statement, consent to act as director and other relevant documents. Lawyers, Judicial Scriveners and Certified Public Accountants can be appointed the agent to apply for registration of incorporation. The registration license tax payable at the time of application is the higher one of either 0.7% of the capital or JPY 150,000.

Q77 会社名を決める際に検討すべきポイントは何ですか。

A 同一住所かつ同一名称の会社が登記されている場合を除いて，基本的にはどのような名前も登記することができます。ただし，不正の目的をもって他の会社であると誤認されるおそれのある会社名を使用することは法令で禁じられています。また，たとえ不正に使用する目的がなくても，広く知られている有名な会社と似た名前を使用することも法令で禁止されています。したがって，他の組織や企業が使用している名前と混同または誤解を招くような名称は避け，他社と明瞭に区分できる名称を登記すべきです。

　会社名は，商人の商号として商業登記され，公衆の閲覧に供されます。同一の本店所在地に，同一の会社名の会社がすでに登記されている場合以外は，自由に商号を登記することができます（商業登記法27条）。

　しかし，たとえ登記できたとしても，不正の目的をもって他の会社であると誤認されるおそれのある商号を使用してはなりません（会社法8条）。不正に使用する目的があれば，たとえ他の会社が有名な会社でなくても違法になります。

　これに対し不正競争防止法は，広く認識されているものと同一もしくは類似の商号を使用して他人の営業と混同させる行為を禁止しています（2条1項1号）。これにより，たとえ不正に使用する目的がなくても，広く知られている有名な会社と似た名前を使用し，それが人々を混同させると判断されれば違法になります。

　そのため，自社と類似する商号がすでに登記されていないかどうかを事前にチェックする必要があります。

Chapter five : 設立手続 Incorporation

Q77 What needs to be considered when naming a new company?

A Any name can be registered unless another company with the same address and the same name is already registered. However, it is legally prohibited to use a company name that may be misidentified as another company for the purpose of fraud. The law also prohibits the use of names similar to widely well-known companies even without the purpose of fraudulent use. Therefore, the name must be distinctive and it must not be misleading or likely to be confused with names used by other organizations and businesses.

The company name is registered as a merchant's business name for public viewing. A company name can be freely registered unless a company with the same name is already registered at the same address (the Commercial Registration Act Article 27).

However, even if you can register, you must not use a name that may be mistaken as another company for the purpose of fraud (the Companies Act Article 8). It is illegal to use the name for the purpose of fraud, even if the other company is not well-known.

On the other hand, the Unfair Competition Prevention Act prohibits the use of a name that is identical or similar to a name that is widely recognized, since it may be confused with other businesses. (Article 2(1)(i). Even if you used the name without intention of fraud, it will still be illegal if you use a name similar to a well-known company and may confuse people.

Therefore, you should check and see if there are any other companies with a similar name to yours before you apply for registration.

207

Q78　定款には何を記載しますか。

A　会社法が選択可能な複数のルールや仕組を提供している場合，定款に記載することで選択適用することができます。その意味で，定款は会社の重要な仕組を決定するルールブックであり，会社の憲法と言えます。設立時に定款を作成しますが，その後定款を変更するには株主総会の特別決議が必要になります。

　定款には，定款で必ず定めなければならない絶対的記載事項，定款で定めることで効力が生じる相対的記載事項，会社法に違反しない範囲で任意に定めることができる任意的記載事項を記載します。

絶対的記載事項

- 目的：会社の事業内容を記載します。記載のない事業を行うことはできません。
- 商号（Q77参照）
- 本店所在地：独立の最小行政区画（市町村または区）を記載すれば良いとされています。
- 設立時の出資額
- 発起人の氏名・住所
- 発行可能株式総数

相対的記載事項の例

- 取締役会の設置の有無（Q24参照）
- 株主総会の決議事項（Q24参照）

Chapter five : 設立手続 Incorporation

Q78 What do the articles of incorporation describe?

A You can choose your rule and structure by stating them in your articles of incorporation, if the Companies Act provides multiple choices. In this sense, the articles of incorporation are company's constitution, a rulebook that determines the important structure of the company. The articles of incorporation are prepared at the time of incorporation. Thereafter, a special resolution of the general meeting of shareholders will be required to change the articles of incorporation.

The articles of incorporation consist of three parts: Absolute matters (compulsory matters to be recorded in the articles of incorporation), Relative matters (matters that will take effect if stated in the articles of incorporation) and Optional matters (you can set forth rules as long as they are in compliance with the Companies Act).

Absolute matters

- Business objectives: a company cannot engage in business which is not listed in business objectives in the articles of incorporation
- Name (See Q77)
- Location of the head office: you don't have to write all the address. Minimum administrative division (city or ward) is enough.
- Value of contributions at incorporation
- Names and addresses of incorporators
- Total number of authorized shares

Relative matters (Samples)

- Establish the board of directors (See Q24)
- What a shareholders' meeting is able to decide (See Q24)

209

- 株式の譲渡を承認する機関（Q66参照）
- 株主総会招集通知の期間短縮（Q29参照）
- 株主総会の決議要件に変更を加える場合（Q31参照）
- 取締役の任期に変更を加える場合（Q33参照）

任意的記載事項の例
- 取締役の員数
- 事業年度
- 株主総会の開催の時期

Chapter five : 設立手続 Incorporation

- Who gives approval to transfer of shares (See Q66)
- Shortened period for notification of convocation of general meeting of shareholders (See Q29)
- Change of the shareholders' meeting resolution requirements (See Q31)
- Change of the office term of directors (See Q33)

Optional matters (Samples)

- Number of directors
- Business year
- When an ordinary shareholders' meeting is held

Q79 登記にはどのような情報が開示されますか。

A 株式会社は，一定の事項を登記し，公衆に対して情報を開示する必要が
あります。主な登記事項は次のとおりです。なお，日本では株主の名前は登
記事項ではありません。

- 目的
- 商号
- 本店所在地
- 資本金の額
- 発行可能株式総数
- 発行済株式の総数
- 公告方法
- 取締役会の設置
- 取締役の氏名
- 代表取締役の氏名・住所
- 監査役の氏名

Chapter five : 設立手続 Incorporation

Q79 What information does the company register disclose?

A K.K. has to disclose certain information to the public through the company register. Major items to be disclosed are as follows. Note that the name of shareholders is not disclosed.

- Business objectives
- Name of the company
- Head office address
- The amount of capital
- Total number of shares authorized to be issued
- The total number of outstanding shares
- Method of public notice
- Whether it has a board of directors
- Name of the directors
- Name and address of the representative directors
- Name of the Corporate Auditor

213

Q80　日本に外資規制はありますか。

A　国家の安全保障に関わる産業など一部の産業への投資や，一定の国からの投資は，事業所管大臣の事前審査が必要になります。それ以外の場合も，事後報告が必要です。

　外国人投資家が対内直接投資を行う場合，外国為替及び外国貿易法（外為法）の規制を受けます 。外国人投資家とは，①非居住者である個人，②外国会社，③非居住者である個人または外国会社の出資比率が50％以上の会社，および④非居住者である個人が取締役の過半数を占める会社をいいます。

　株式会社の株式を外国人投資家が取得する場合には規制対象になります。ただし，株式会社が上場企業の場合は，出資比率が10％以上になるものが対象になります。合同会社の場合も同様に，その持分を外国人投資家が取得する場合には対内直接投資に該当します。外国会社の支店を設置する場合，たとえ本店から支店に資金を拠出しない場合でも対内直接投資に該当します。

　国家の安全保障に関わる産業（告示別表第一），農業や伝統工芸，電気やガスなどの公共事業など一部の産業分野（告示別表第二）への投資は事業所管大臣の事前審査が必要になります。また，一定の国からの投資についても事業所管大臣の事前審査が必要になります。それ以外のほとんどの場合は，事業所管大臣への事後報告のみが課せられています。事後報告はいわゆる外資規制ではありませんが，報告を失念しないよう気をつけなければなりません。

　そのほか，個別の業法によって外資に対して出資規制が設けられている場合

214

Chapter five：設立手続 Incorporation

Q80　Does Japan have foreign investment restrictions?

A　Investment in certain industries including national security and investment from certain countries will require prior review by the relevant minister. In other cases, you are required to submit a report after investment.

Inward direct investment by foreign investors is subject to the regulation of the Foreign Exchange and Foreign Trade Act. Foreign investors are defined as 1) a nonresident individual, 2) a foreign company, 3) a domestic company with 50% or more of the shares held by nonresident individuals and/or foreign companies, and 4) a domestic company of which a majority of directors are nonresident.

Acquiring shares of K.K. by foreign investors is subject to foreign investment restrictions unless K.K. is a listed company and their shareholding by a foreign investor is less than 10%. Foreign investment in G.K. is also subject to the regulation. Establishing a branch office of a foreign corporation is deemed as the inward direct investment, even if it does not contribute funds from the head office to the branch office.

Foreign investors who wish to invest in certain defense-related industries (Notification Appendix Table 1), certain industries including agriculture, traditional crafts, and public services such as electricity and gas (Notification Appendix Table 2) are required to apply for the preliminary examination conducted by the relevant minister. Investments from particular countries are also subject to the preliminary examination. If your industry is out of scope of examination, which mostly is the case, you are only required to report to the minister after the investment is executed. Reporting is an important obligation.

In addition, there are some laws which impose restrictions on shareholding

215

があります。例えば，外資比率が3分の1以上の会社は航空法によって航空運送事業の許可を受けることができないとされています。同様の免許規制は，電波法によるテレビ局，貨物利用運送事業法による運送会社などに課せられています。

Chapter five：設立手続 Incorporation

by foreign investors. For example, a company with a foreign capital ratio of more than one third is not permitted to receive a business license for air transport business under the aeronautical laws. Similar licensing restrictions are imposed on television stations under the Radio Laws, shipping companies under the Freight Utilization Transport Business Laws.

▶▶合同会社

Q81 最低社員数および最低資本金の規制はありますか。

A 株式会社の場合と同様に，合同会社の設立準拠法である会社法は，社員数および資本金に制限を設けていません。そのため，社員1名，資本金1円の合同会社を設立することができます。

しかしながら，本国からの駐在員の在留資格（ビザ）を申請する場合など一定の資本金が必要となる場合があります。また，日本円でしか資本金の登記はできません。

Chapter five：設立手続 Incorporation

Q81 Are there minimum requirements for the capital amount and the number of members?

A The companies Act, the law governing incorporation of G.K., has no minimum requirements for the capital amount and the number of members. So, you can set up a company with a capital of JPY 1 and one member.

However, you may be required to have certain amount of capital in some situations, such as when applying for the status of residence (Visa) for expatriates. Japanese yen is the only currency allowed for capital registration.

Q82 合同会社の設立の流れについて教えてください。

A 3つのステップがあります。まず，社員となる予定の者が発起人となり，定款を作成します。次に，発起人は出資を履行して社員になります。最後に法務局に対して設立登記の申請を行います。

ステップ1：定款の作成

　定款の作成方法は概ね株式会社の場合と同じです。ただし，株式会社とは異なり，定款は公証人の認証を受ける必要はありません。

ステップ2：出資の履行

　有限責任制度を採用しているため，設立前に出資を払い込む必要があります。株式会社の場合，払込は銀行で行うこととされているため（会社法34条），通帳の写しの提出が必要になりますが，合同会社の場合は銀行での払込は要求されていません（会社法578条）。そのため，出資が確実に行われたことを証明する書類として，合同会社が社員にあてて発行した出資金領収書の写しを設立登記の際に法務局に提出します。

ステップ3：設立登記

　法務局に対して設立登記の申請は社員が行います。定款，出資金領収書など必要書類を添えて申請します。弁護士，司法書士および公認会計士による代理申請が認められています。申請時に登録免許税を納付します。登録免許税は，資本金の0.7%と6万円のいずれか高いほうとされています。

220

Chapter five：設立手続 Incorporation

Q82　What are the steps to incorporating G.K.?

A　Incorporating G.K. is a three-step process. 1) person(s) who wishes to become a member of the G.K. is appointed as an incorporator(s) called "hokkinin" and prepares the articles of incorporation. 2) the incorporator(s) make contributions to the company to become a member. 3) a member applies for registration of establishment with the Legal Affairs Bureau.

Step1: Completing articles of incorporation

The articles of incorporation are prepared almost the same way as K.K. However, it dose not require to be notarized by a notary public.

Step2: Contribution

As G.K. adopts limited liability, proposed members must make contributions before incorporation.

In the case of K.K., contributions must be made at a bank account (the Companies Act Article 34), and a copy of the bank statement must be submitted to the authority. On the contrary, G.K.'s contributions are not required to be made in a bank account (Article 578). Therefore, instead of bank statements, a copy of the receipt issued by G.K. will be submitted to the authority to prove that the contribution has been completed.

Step3: Registration

Finally, a member applies for registration of establishment with the Legal Affairs Bureau, by submitting articles of incorporation, a copy of the receipt and other relevant documents. Lawyers, Judicial Scriveners and Certified Public Accountants can be appointed as the agent to apply for registration of incorporation. The registration license tax payable at the time of application is the higher one of either 0.7% of the capital or JPY 60,000.

221

▶▶支　店

Q83　支店の登記の流れについて教えてください。

A　外国会社の日本支店の設置に関する宣誓供述書を作成し，法務局に対して外国会社の登記の申請を行います。

　新たな法人を設立するわけではないので，定款の作成や資本金の払込は不要です。日本における代表者を定めて必要事項を登記します。営業所が設置されていれば営業所の住所も登記します。そのほか，日本における同種の会社または最も類似する会社の設立登記の登記事項に準ずる事項を登記します。例えば，外国会社の形態が日本の株式会社に最も類似する場合には，代表取締役の氏名および住所など株式会社に求められる登記事項を登記します。

　登記に必要な資料として，以下のものがあります。
- 本店の存在を認めるに足りる書面（法人資格証明書など）
- 外国会社の日本における代表者が適法に選任されたことを証する書面（任命書など）
- 定款または外国会社の性質を識別するに足りる書面
- 公告方法についての定めを証する書面

　本国の管轄官庁の証明書以外の書類は，本国の管轄官庁または日本における領事その他権限がある官憲の認証を受けたものでなければなりません。これらの書類を準備するのは実務上非常に煩雑なので，日本における代表者が上記の事項を宣誓した宣誓供述書に本国の領事等が認証したものおよびその訳文を提出することが認められています。

Chapter five：設立手続 Incorporation

Q83 How do I register Japan branch of foreign corporation?

A Prepare an affidavit regarding a Japan branch of a foreign company, and apply for registration with the Legal Affairs Bureau.

Registering a Japan branch is not establishing a new corporation. Therefore, there is no need to prepare articles of incorporation or pay contributions. A foreign company will appoint a representative(s) of Japan and register the necessary information. If the foreign company sets up an actual office in Japan, the address of the office will also be registered. In addition, a foreign company needs to disclose the matters that the same kind or the most similar kind of the company in Japan. For example, if the form of the foreign company is most similar to a Japanese K.K., the foreign company would need to register name and address of their representative directors, which are required of K.K.

The following materials are required for registration.

- Document to prove the existence of the foreign company's head office (ex. certified copy of the commercial register in the home country)
- Document certifying the legality of the appointment of the representative in Japan (ex. letter of appointment)
- Articles of incorporation or document which show the features of the foreign company
- Document certifying the method of public notice

Documents other than certificates issued by the government bodies must be certified by the authority of the country, Consul in Japan, or other authorized officials. Such preparation is very time consuming. So, it is acceptable for the representative of Japan to submit an affidavit stating the matters above, with it certified by the consul of the home country, and its translation.

223

Chapter 6

現地税制
Local Taxation

Q84 法人税の概要について教えてください。

A 法人の所得には5つの税金が課せられます。国税である法人税および地方法人税，地方税である法人住民税，法人事業税および地方法人特別税（2020年12月期から特別法人事業税）が課税されます。そのうち，事業税および地方法人特別税は支払時に損金となるため，実効税率は各税率の単純合計より低くなります。税率は所在地や規模などにより変わりますが，東京の中小企業の2019年12月期の実効税率は約33％です。

東京にある会社の税率は次のとおりです。

①外形標準課税（Q10参照）の適用がある大企業

	2019年12月期	2020年12月期
法人税率	23.20％	23.20％
地方法人税率	（4.4％） 1.02％	（10.3％） 2.39％
法人住民税率	（16.3％） 3.78％	（10.4％） 2.41％
法人事業税	0.88％	1.18％
地方法人特別税 （特別法人事業税）	2.90％	2.60％
合計	31.78％	31.78％
実効税率	30.62％	30.62％

Chapter six：現地税制 Local Taxation

Q84 What taxes will be imposed on corporate incomes?

A Corporate incomes are subject to 5 taxes: Corporation Tax and Local Corporation Tax as national taxes, Corporation Inhabitant Tax, Corporation Business Tax and Local Corporation Special Tax (from FY Dec 2019, Special Corporation Business Tax) as local government taxes. Among them, business tax and local corporation special tax are fully tax deductible at the payment. As such, the effective tax rate is lower than the total of headline tax rates. The tax rate varies depending on the location and size. The effective tax rate for SMEs in Tokyo for the fiscal year ending December 2019 is approximately 33%.

Here is a table of tax rate for companies in Tokyo.

1) Large enterprise subject to Size-Based Business Tax (See Q10)

	FY Dec 2019	FY Dec 2020
Corporation Tax	23.20%	23.20%
Local Corporation Tax (surtax)	(4.4%) 1.02%	(10.3%) 2.39%
Inhabitant Tax (surtax)	(16.3%) 3.78%	(10.4%) 2.41%
Business Tax	0.88%	1.18%
Local Corporation Special Tax (Special Corporation Business Tax)	2.90%	2.60%
Total rate	31.78%	31.78%
Effective tax rate	30.62%	30.62%

227

②中小企業

	2019年12月期	2020年12月期
法人税率	23.20％	23.20％
地方法人税率	(4.4％) 1.02％	(10.3％) 2.39％
法人住民税率※	(12.9％) 2.99％	(7.0％) 1.62％
法人事業税※	6.70％	7.00％
地方法人特別税 （特別法人事業税）	2.89％	2.59％
合計	36.81％	36.80％
実効税率	33.59％	33.58％

※超過税率の適用なし

　全世界課税が採用されており，外国支店の利益などの国外源泉所得も課税対象になります。ただし，25％以上の株式を保有する外国関連会社からの配当は，95％が免税されます。

　申告期限は決算日から2カ月以内ですが，1カ月（会計監査人設置会社は最大で4カ月）の申告期限延長が可能です。ただし，延滞税がかかるため，実務では2カ月以内に見込額を納付しておきます。

　中間納付は，中間決算に基づいて中間申告を行うか，または前年度の法人税額の半額を納付します。設立初年度である場合，または前年度の法人税額が20万円以下の場合には中間納付は不要です。

Chapter six : 現地税制 Local Taxation

2) SME

	FY Dec 2019	FY Dec 2020
Corporation Tax	23.20%	23.20%
Local Corporation Tax (surtax)	(4.4%) 1.02%	(10.3%) 2.39%
Inhabitant Tax (surtax)※	(12.9%) 2.99%	(7.0%) 1.62%
Business Tax※	6.70%	7.00%
Local Corporation Special Tax (Special Corporation Business Tax)	2.89%	2.59%
Total rate	36.81%	36.80%
Effective tax rate	33.59%	33.58%

※For companies that are exempt from Excess tax rate

As worldwide income is taxable, foreign sourced incomes including profits earned by a foreign branch are subject to corporate income tax. However, 95% of the foreign dividends from foreign affiliate companies are exempted from taxation.

Tax deadline for filing is two months after the fiscal year end. 1-month extension is available (up to 4-month extension can be granted to companies with external auditor). In practice, you will pay the estimated tax amount within two months because interest will be incurred when you pay after the original deadline even if you are granted extension.

You will receive an interim tax bill charging half the tax amount of last year unless you submit a half year tax return based on half year financials. Interim tax payment is required if it is the first fiscal year since incorporation, or if the tax amount of the previous year was 200,000 yen or less.

229

Q85 消費税はどのような税制ですか。

A 消費税とは，日本国内における物品およびサービスの提供ならびに物品の輸入に対して課される付加価値税です。税率は 8 ％（2019年10月から10%）で，1,000万円超の売上がある事業者は消費税課税事業者として登録する義務があります。

消費税課税事業者は物品およびサービスの売上に対して消費税を徴収する一方，ビジネスに関連する物品およびサービスの仕入において支払った消費税を控除することができます。

税率は消費税6.3％と地方消費税1.7％の合計 8 ％ですが，2019年10月から消費税7.8％と地方消費税2.2％の合計10%に引き上げられます。

法人は決算日から 2 カ月以内に申告と納税を行います。課税対象期間を 1 年から 3 カ月または 1 カ月に短縮することができます。消費税の還付を受ける場合には資金繰りが助かりますが，最低 2 年間は再変更することができないので慎重に検討すべきです。

基本的には 2 年前の課税売上が1,000万円以下であれば消費税の納税が免除されます（Q86参照）。免税事業者は課税当局に消費税を納付する義務を免除されますが，販売先に消費税を請求することは禁じられていません。これにより免税事業者はいわゆる益税が得られていました。これに対し，2023年10月からはインボイス方式が導入されるため，免税事業者は販売先に対して消費税を請求することができなくなります。インボイス方式が導入されると，消費税事業者番号を記載した請求書を発行しなければ消費税を徴収できなくなるからです。

Chapter six : 現地税制 Local Taxation

Q85 What is Consumption tax?

A Consumption tax, or C-tax, is a value added tax, levied on the sales of goods and services in Japan and imports to Japan. The tax rate is 8% (10% from Oct 2019), and Business owners with a turnover of more than JPY 10 million must apply for C-tax register.

C-tax-registered businesses must charge C-tax on their goods or services and they may reclaim C-tax they've paid on business related goods or services.

The tax rate is currently 6.3% for national tax and 1.7% for local government tax, which will be increased up to 7.8% and 2.2% from October 2019 respectively.

Corporations must file a C-tax return within 2 months after their fiscal year end. Tax period can be shortened from 1 year to 3 months or 1 month, which may help with your cash flow if you expect refunds. Note that once you change the tax period, you can't change it again at least for two years.

Basically, if your turnover two years ago was JPY 10 million or less, you are exempted from C-tax registration (See Q86). Currently, non-registered businesses are not prohibited to charge C-tax on their goods and services. As a result, non-registered businesses are able to gain a kind of tax benefits. From October 2023, tax invoice system will be introduced and tax-registered number needs to be described on the sales invoices for C-tax charge. Therefore, non-registered businesses will not be allowed to charge C-tax.

231

Q86　消費税の課税事業者となる要件は何ですか。

A　前々事業年度の課税売上高が1,000万円を超えると課税事業者として登録しなければなりません。また，前事業年度の上半期の課税売上高が1,000万円を超える場合も登録義務が発生しますが，同期間の給与が1,000万円を超えていなければ免除されます。設立から２年間は，資本金が1,000万円以上である場合，または親会社の前々事業年度の課税売上高が５億円を超えている場合に，課税事業者となります。

消費税の課税事業者となる要件は次のとおりです。

①　前々事業年度（基準期間）の課税売上高が1,000万円超

②　前事業の上半期（特定期間）の課税売上高が1,000万円超（同期間の給与が1,000万円を超えていなければ免除）

③　資本金が1,000万円以上

④　株式の50％超を直接または間接に保有する株主の前々事業年度における課税売上高が５億円超

　設立１期目は，要件③④で，設立２期目は，要件②③④で判定します。設立３期目以降は，要件①②で判定します。要件④について，日本子会社を設立する前から外国親会社が日本に輸出していたとしても，国外取引として課税売上高には該当しないため，要件④には該当しません。したがって，設立初年度は

232

Chapter six：現地税制 Local Taxation

Q86 What are C-tax registration thresholds?

A A business owner must register for C-tax, if its taxable turnover in the year before preceding taxable year is more than JPY 10 million. If a company's taxable turnover in the first half period of preceding year exceeds JPY 10 million, the company also needs to register for C-tax, unless its personal expenses during the same period do not exceed JPY 10 million. For the first two years from incorporation, a company must register if its capital is JPY 10 million or more, or if its parent company earned a taxable turnover of more than JPY 500 million in the year before preceding taxable year.

Requirements for compulsory registrations are as follows.

1) taxable turnover in the year before preceding taxable year is more than JPY 10 million
2) taxable turnover in the first half period of preceding year exceeds JPY 10 million (unless personal expenses during the same period does not exceed JPY 10 million)
3) capital is JPY 10 million or more
4) a shareholder who directly or indirectly holds more than 50% of the shares earned a taxable turnover of more than JPY 500 million in the year before preceding taxable year

For the first year from incorporation, it is determined by the requirement 3) and 4). For the second year, 2), 3) and 4) are applied, and for the third year and after, it will be judged by 1) and 2). As for 4), even if the foreign parent company had exported its goods and services to Japan before incorporation of its Japan subsidiary, it does not fall under 4) because exporting counts as

233

資本金が1,000万円未満であれば免税事業者となるのが通常です。

　日本支店を設立する場合，外国会社について判定を行います。そのため，日本支店の設置初年度であっても通常は「設立3期目以降」で判定することになります。従前から本店が日本に輸出していたとしても，国外取引として課税売上高には該当しないため，設置初年度は免税事業者になります。

Chapter six : 現地税制 Local Taxation

out-of-scope supplies, not as taxable turnover.

In the case of setting up a Japan branch, the same conditions are applied to the foreign company. Therefore, conditions for the third year and after are usually applied even for the first year of the Japan branch. Even if the head office of the foreign company had exported its goods and services to Japan previously, the Japan branch is exempted from C-tax registration, because exporting counts as out-of-scope supplies, not as taxable turnover.

Q87　日本ではどのような取引に源泉所得税が課せられますか。

A　従業員に対する給与，弁護士など個人のプロフェッショナルに対する報酬，配当・利子，非居住者または外国会社に対するロイヤルティ支払などが源泉所得の対象になります。

主な源泉対象取引は以下のとおりです。

①　従業員および役員に対する給与および退職金の支払

②　弁護士，公認会計士，翻訳家など個人プロフェッショナルに対する報酬

③　配当および預金利息

④　非居住者または外国会社に支払うロイヤルティ，貸付金利息，人的役務の提供の対価，不動産賃料など

支払を行った月の翌月10日までに申告および納付を行います。給与の支給人員が常時10人未満の小規模事業者は，上記①および②について年2回にまとめて納付することが認められています。

非居住者または外国会社に対する支払は，ロイヤルティ，人的役務の提供の対価，不動産賃料など，居住者および内国法人と比べて広範囲な範囲で源泉税が課されます。国内法の主な税率は，配当20.42％，利子15.315％，ロイヤルティ20.42％ですが，租税条約に上限税率が定められている場合があります。租税条約の適用にあたっては税務署へ届け出る必要があります。

ところで，外国会社の日本支店に対する上記④の支払も源泉徴収の対象となりますが，日本で税務申告を行っている点では内国法人と変わらないため，上記④の支払について源泉免除証明書の交付を受けることができます。源泉免除証明書の提示を受けた支払者は源泉徴収義務が免除されます。

Chapter six : 現地税制 Local Taxation

Q87 What payments are subject to withholding tax in Japan?

A Withholding tax applies to salaries paid to employees, service fees to individual professionals such as lawyers, dividends and interests, and certain payments to nonresidents and foreign companies including loyalty.

Major taxable transactions are as follows:

1) salaries paid to employees and fees paid to directors
2) service fees to individual professionals such as lawyers, CPAs and translators
3) dividends and bank interests
4) royalties, interests and fees for personal services that are paid to non-residents and foreign corporations

Withholding tax filing and tax payments are due on the 10th of the next month from the date of payment. Small businesses with less than 10 employees can apply for the extension for the payment of 1) and 2). You will file and pay twice a year.

When you make payments to non-residents and foreign corporations, withholding tax will be imposed on wider range of transactions than residents and domestic corporations, including royalties, interests and fees for personal services. Domestic tax law sets out 20.42% on dividends and loyalty, and 15.315% on interests. Tax treaties may have upper limits on tax rates. You would need to submit an application if you want to use a tax treaty.

Payments of the above 4) made to Japan branches of foreign corporations are also subject to withholding tax. Since branches submit tax returns in the same way as domestic corporations, branches can apply for exemptions and obtain certificates to show payers to release withholding obligation.

237

【著者紹介】

三宅　周兵（みやけ・しゅうへい）

公認会計士・税理士

株式会社ナヴィスコンサルティング 代表取締役

外資系企業に対して税務アドバイス及びアウトソーシングを提供し，日本進出を支援している。また，内外のクライアントに対してM&Aアドバイザリー，海外進出支援，企業オーナーや外国人の相続対策を数多く手がけている。

1999年	慶応義塾大学環境情報学部卒業
	富士銀行（現 みずほ銀行）入行
2003年	公認会計士2次試験合格
	優成監査法人（現 太陽有限責任監査法人）入所
2011年	Crowe Horwath First Trust（Singapore）LLP 出向
2013年	優成監査法人（現 太陽有限責任監査法人）パートナー
2015年	株式会社ナヴィスコンサルティング 代表取締役（現任）

Author biography

Joey Shuhei MIYAKE is a Certified Public Accountant (CPA) and the founder and CEO of Navis Consulting. He has devoted himself to supporting foreign corporations to start a business in Japan, providing tax advice and outsourcing services. He also provides international corporations with M&A advisory, overseas business support, and inheritance tax planning for business owners and expatriates.

2015-Present   CEO, Navis Consulting Co., Ltd.

2013   Partner, Yusei Audit & Co. (Grant Thornton)

2011   Crowe Horwath First Trust (Singapore) LLP

2003   Yusei Audit & Co. (Grant Thornton)

2003   Certified to Practice in Japan

1999   The Fuji Bank, Limited (Mizuho Bank, Ltd.)

1999   Keio University, Faculty of Environmental Information

和英対照
インバウンド会社設立ガイド

2019年12月15日　第1版第1刷発行

著　者　三　宅　周　兵
発行者　山　本　　継
発行所　㈱中央経済社
発売元　㈱中央経済グループ
　　　　パ ブ リ ッ シ ン グ

〒101-0051　東京都千代田区神田神保町1-31-2
電　話　03 (3293) 3371 (編集代表)
　　　　03 (3293) 3381 (営業代表)
http://www.chuokeizai.co.jp/
製　版／三英グラフィック・アーツ㈱

© 2019
Printed in Japan

印　刷／三　英　印　刷　㈱
製　本／㈲井　上　製　本　所

＊頁の「欠落」や「順序違い」などがありましたらお取り替えいた
しますので発売元までご送付ください。(送料小社負担)

ISBN978-4-502-32221-1　C3034

JCOPY〈出版者著作権管理機構委託出版物〉本書を無断で複写複製(コピー)することは,
著作権法上の例外を除き,禁じられています。本書をコピーされる場合は事前に出版者
著作権管理機構 (JCOPY) の許諾を受けてください。
JCOPY〈http://www.jcopy.or.jp　e メール：info@jcopy.or.jp〉

●着眼力シリーズ●

税務調査官の着眼力Ⅱ
間違いだらけの相続税対策
秋山清成著

テレビや小説ではわからないウソみたいな本当の話にとにかく驚くばかり！　遺言どおりに相続できない？／とりあえず、もしもに備えて、納税資金の確保が最優先です／相続放棄で身を守る？／遺言書が存在する相続ほどこじれる？　ほか

女性社労士の着眼力
知ったかぶりの社会保険
田島雅子著

マイナンバーで迫られる社会保険の加入問題。経営者なら、従業員を厚生年金に加入させ半額を会社負担とするか、個人事業主で国民年金とするか？　配偶者なら、保険料を納めず第3号被保険者でいるか、所得制限のない年金保険加入者になるか？

アセットマネジャーの着眼力
間違いだらけの不動産投資
佐々木重徳著

節税ありきの不動産投資でいいんですか？安易な判断が命取りになりますよ！　相続税対策でドツボに嵌るアパート経営／高利回り物件って、ホントにお得なの？／意外と奥が深いワンルームマンション投資／リノベーションあれこれ　ほか

中央経済社